CW01082115

World Without End?

Contours of a Post-Terrorism World

Leslie Griffiths and Jennifer Potter

✠ EPWORTH

Copyright © Leslie Griffiths and Jennifer Potter 2007

The Authors have asserted their right under the Copyright, Designs and
Patents Act, 1988, to be identified as the Authors of this Work

British Library Cataloguing in Publication data

A catalogue record for this book is available
from the British Library

978 0 7162 0608 8

First published in 2007
by Epworth
4 John Wesley Road
Werrington
Peterborough PE4 6ZP

Typeset by Regent Typesetting, London
Printed and bound in Great Britain by
William Clowes Ltd, Beccles, Suffolk

Contents

Foreword

This is an important book. I doubt very much whether Leslie Griffiths or Jennifer Potter is afflicted by pride but they are entitled to feel proud of it.

I started reading *World without End? Contours of a Post-Terrorism World* by the Tiber, just across the road from Rome's great synagogue. Rome is a city of contradictions that prompt me to think more carefully. It is rich in religious life, with over 400 Catholic churches. The kids whizzing by on their Lambrettas make a point of displaying their hedonism; talk to them and they make a point of being explicitly secular. And this synagogue is now a museum. Its former congregation went to the gas chambers, usually having been rounded up by their Christian neighbours.

These observations demonstrate the ambivalence I feel when trying to grasp the role of religion in the analysis of momentous political events. There are always alternative sources of political thought, and why should religious leaders have something very special to say? We look to spiritual thinkers for special insights about peace and reconciliation because they lie at the heart of their religious concepts. Yet we live in a period where belligerence and violence based on religious belief appear to be growing. Violence and hostile language are often 'sanitized' by some bolt-on reference to a holy text as justification for an extreme act or policy. So I am delighted to read a book that follows a wholly different path and avoids all such sophistry.

First, Leslie Griffiths and Jennifer Potter draw on their scholarship, experience and straightforward humanity to understand how biblical writers grasped dynamic change in their own time, how those authors handled change, threats and confusion, and how this is manifest in what they wrote in biblical text. I had certainly not appreciated the extent to which theological and political revision was needed to make sense of past events and beliefs in changed circumstances, or the sophistication of the intellectual processes. But, then, most of us are not taught to read biblical texts that way.

Consequently, Griffiths and Potter never themselves try to apply mechanical lessons from one time and context to a completely different one. Rather, they draw on the creativity of the methods they detect and display in the world of earlier commentators.

Next, they employ the same qualities of innovation and analysis to six international studies involving conflict and the most disagreeable experiences of globalization. Here, they draw on study and first-hand knowledge of some of the extremely difficult places in which they conducted their ministry. Their selection makes great sense because none of the problems they consider could possibly be solved on the basis of what any nation state can do on its own, however powerful that state. The deaths and denigration, the communities butchered, the women trafficked, the people robbed of everything so systematically that they starved – each makes us think: 'What could the UK have done to stop that crime?' And while the answer will often be we should do more, we also understand that even the UK doing more will not work. Nor does the unilateral action of the world's remaining hyperpower.

In respect of each case it is imperative to have effective international institutions to address international crimes, crises and their causes.

Of course, we do have international institutions on which we would like to rely. Yet it cannot really be said that they are effective in today's world. They were for the most part designed to aid post-World War Two recovery or to manage and mediate Cold War tensions and nuclear threats. In a sense, they did a significant job relatively successfully. But that world has passed and this book raises key questions for the present rather than the past. The vital institutions – the United Nations and the Bretton Woods financial organizations – need, in my view, fundamental re-engineering precisely because they are vital to us but cannot do the job we need.

For example, to focus on the UN, Kofi Annan set out in stark terms the need for the organization to deal with humanitarian disaster effectively even if this breached any individual state's sovereignty. The responsibility to protect people from crimes against humanity arises in its sharpest form when it is the government of those very people that commits or colludes in the crimes. The UN adopted the obligation to protect, but remains consistently frustrated when a rapid intervention is needed.

Vetoes and truculent non-cooperation in the Security Council still have the ring of the Cold War about them, however desperate the circumstances. Old Cold War client states, like Sudan, are shielded from the consequences of actions that will cost millions more lives. The new Human Rights Council has yet to demonstrate that its commitment to human rights is more purposeful than that of its predecessors.

And Kofi Annan simply could not get agreement to efficient, accountable and transparent machinery. You cannot mobilize the best human and appropriate financial resources, and then manage them well, if your organization is barely fit for purpose.

In 2005 Annan identified these problems at the UN World Summit in *In Larger Freedom*. The UK supported him vigorously. Jack Straw (then Foreign Secretary) and Hilary Benn (Secretary of State for International Development) emphasized freedom from want and fear, and the right to live in dignity as inspirational goals. Jack Straw led our strategic re-prioritization and work on the architecture to deliver priorities. Our collective inability to move many UN members beyond the narrowest of state interests and what amounts to an atavistic adherence to Cold War stand-offs tempers my sense of pride in this.

So I share the Griffiths-Potter thesis. If we fail to understand global trends, international work will fail. We must respect cultural, religious and ethnic variety, but we also have more universal obligations. And that is why international organizations must be fit for purpose. They are the best instruments to bridge our differences and they must be made to work. Our new analysis has to break free of the thinking that dominated the early period of the UN, the International Monetary Fund and so on.

Reading this book on the banks of the Tiber, I truly welcome the clarity of political insight brought to us by two fine theologians.

David Triesman
Lord Triesman of Tottenham
Parliamentary Under-Secretary of State
Foreign and Commonwealth Office
March 2007

1

The End of an Age

The group of demonstrators who left the Wesley's Chapel Manse on 15 February 2003, armed with banners, fired up with indignation, were in high spirits as they moved off to join the hundreds of thousands of others moving towards central London. Those left behind were torn – full of admiration for the youngsters' enthusiasm and idealism, full of self-questioning and deep uncertainty about the issue that had led them forth.

As we looked into ourselves and reflected on our own anxieties, we came to see that this moment in history represents something of a crossroads. It's a time of 'paradigm shift', a moment of radical transition, when a great number of the landmarks that have given the world its bearings in the period following World War II are being swept away. And nobody is quite certain what will replace them.

Such moments breed anxiety. And anxiety brings forth its own 'prophets' and 'healers'. Apocalyptic pronouncements abound, quick fixes and short-cut solutions are everywhere on offer, a babble of opinion is heard on all sides.

How do we read the signs of these times? How do we make sense of a world being shaken to its foundations? What have Christians to offer at such times? Can Christian thinkers shake themselves free from a domestic agenda dominated by constant tinkering with ecclesiastical reorganization or else an obsessive preoccupation with various aspects of sexuality in order to address the great questions of our day? We reflected long and hard and this little book is an attempt to share some of the thinking of two people who've wrestled with these issues. We dare to hope that these pages may generate a lively and healthy discussion.

So much happened in that *fin-de-siècle* decade. It was a period that lasted longer than ten years, of course. Indeed, it ran roughly from 1987 to 2001! This longer version of the decade saw such extraordinary events pile up on one another. In politics, in finance, in philosophy and theology, in the movement of peoples and capital, everything seemed to be changing. Countries as well as concepts.

They fell like dominoes. Czechoslovakia, Hungary, Romania, Bulgaria, Poland, East Germany, Lithuania, Estonia, Latvia – until the Warsaw Pact was no more. Then came the internal and often quiet revolutions in Ukraine, Georgia and other Soviet Republics around the Black Sea. The USSR was no more. Mikhail Gorbachev who, with his policies of *perestroika*, and *glasnost* had let the genie out of the bottle, was himself swept away by events. Under Boris Yeltsin, Russia went through one travail after another. The collapse of their much-famed army, the erosion of the authority of the KGB, the massive speculative bids for the country's natural resources, the scam banking enterprises, the collapse of traditional life – all these developments saw Russia itself implode.

Nor were these problems restricted to the territories that had constituted the former USSR. In places much further afield there were repercussions of a radical nature. For years, 'surrogate wars' had been fought between East and West as, for example, in Mozambique. No better illustration of the futility of such enterprises could be offered than the example of a young Mozambican who'd been taken out of high school in his late teens and sent to Russia to be trained as a MIG-15 pilot. His stay there lasted several years and the sole skill he acquired was to fly fighter planes on behalf of the Soviet-backed government in Maputo against 'rebel forces' within his own country. That is, he'd been lavishly equipped to kill his own people. The Renamo/Frelimo civil war ended only with the collapse of communism, just as this young man was returning to do his deadly work. He was redundant before he arrived!

It was a similar tale in Ethiopia where a fierce struggle had been taking place for many years and in a way that often bewildered outside commentators. The government in Addis Ababa, backed first by

Washington and then by the Warsaw Pact, was able to attract formidable amounts of armoury and weaponry. One of the uses to which it put these arms was to oppose those seeking independence for its Eritrean province. Once again, it took the cataclysmic events that surrounded the fall of the old order to allow a solution to emerge from that part of Africa.

With the departure of people like Honecker and Ceauşescu, the collapse of organizations like the KGB and the Stasi, and (ultimate icon of those heady days) the pulling down of the Berlin Wall, it was clear that we were witnessing far more than a mere change of regime. This was the end of an era. We were witnessing the emergence of a new world order. So many of the geo-political factors that had been in place since the end of the Second World War were swept away. A bipolar world with each side of the dialectic in a fixed position against the other had disappeared for ever. The iron curtain that, in Winston Churchill's words, had descended on Europe had now been pulled aside. The way was now open for Europe to redefine itself. Russia would be destined to spend some years of uncertainty regathering its forces. Its grip on Afghanistan (where it had spent so many fruitless years and invested so much effort in trying to establish its hegemony) was loosened. It would continue to be troubled by the violent insurgencies of Chechnya and other Islamic republics on its south-eastern flank.

And on the other side of this equation would emerge a new America – no longer fixated on its ancient oppositions to world communism but, like any old drug addict, still needing to supply its habit. A new enemy would be needed to replace the old. The world of Islam loomed large among the possible candidates.

The end of the Cold War was one, but only one, of the key factors that ushered in this new era. So radical were the forces unleashed and so different were the factors now in play that the only adequate way of describing these events would be to call them a 'paradigm shift'. The rules of the game had been changed, familiar landmarks had been swept away, new players had been introduced, a re-alignment of forces was under way. And we'd have to think of new ways to establish our place in the world.

At this turning point in our recent history two very significant events took place in widely separated parts of the world. The first was in South Africa where we witnessed the culmination of decades of protest against the apartheid policies of successive nationalist governments. The dénouement arrived in a great rush in the very first years of the new decade. Nothing had captured the world's need for a 'righteous cause' more than the plight of South Africa's black and coloured populations. There had been boycotts and demonstrations and international protest galore. Great sporting events had been marked by radical action and, one way or another, South Africa had become a pariah state. The tide began to turn in the late 1980s and the whole world was amazed to see President de Klerk come forward with his own version of *glasnost* and *perestroika*. This led to the unbanning of the African National Congress and, in March 1991, the freeing of Nelson Mandela from the prison cell in which he had languished for over a quarter of a century. There was great euphoria at this event and many of us remember rushing home from church that Sunday morning to witness the emergence of the great Mandela from the shackles of his imprisonment. Soon the movement became unstoppable and the 1994 elections, with televised pictures of endless snakes of people lined up simply for the privilege of voting, gave us images that were as striking as those showing the destruction of the Berlin Wall. Perhaps a new and more positive era had arrived! This South African revolution had thrown up some larger-than-life personalities – Joe Slovo, Steve Biko, the inimitable Desmond Tutu and the unique Nelson Mandela himself. And now, of course, the forces that for so long had been concentrated on saying NO to apartheid needed to reorganize themselves around the imperative to build a new nation. Sometimes it is much harder to construct than to destroy. South Africa was about to discover the realities of living in the complicated new world that had come into being during the many years of its purdah.

The second great event of these years was of a different order altogether. In 1991 the First Gulf War saw the forces of the West pitted against the Republican Guard of Iraq's dictator Saddam Hussein. He had seemed able almost literally to get away with murder for so long. After all, he had been backed by the West as their 'safe man' against the perceived tyranny of the Islamic state of Iran where Ayatollah Khomeini had succeeded the ousted Shah as long ago as 1976. Saddam Hussein had provoked an unnecessary and costly war against Iran in which almost a million people died. In order to quell the rebellious Kurds within his territory he had developed chemical weapons that he had not hesitated to use. And, another act of social control, he drained the marshlands to the south of Iraq in order to drive the Marsh Arabs (Shi'a Muslims) from their traditional environment. It was cynical and calculated and drew strength in no small measure from the impunity he felt as the West's favoured person in Middle East politics where so much that happened was as shifting as its desert sands.

When Saddam Hussein put his foot across the Kuwaiti border, however, he went too far. He'd long since become an embarrassment but now he'd given the outside world an excuse to retaliate. It was ironic that the American government that took the lead in the First Gulf War should have been under the leadership of President George Bush Senior. Subsequent studies have shown an intricate set of relationships between the Bush clan and the ruling family of Saudi Arabia. It's clear that Bush had a mixture of motives for welcoming the chance to render Saddam Hussein's regime impotent. The war was brief and decisive. The much-vaunted Republican Guard turned and fled. Lessons that might have been useful ten years later were being offered.

Many commentators were heard wondering whether Bush should have 'finished the job off' in 1991, among them the unlikely voice of Neil Kinnock. He'd been leader of the Labour opposition in the British parliament at the time and had pleaded with the American President to complete the action, knowing that, if he didn't, it would come back to haunt us.

The First Gulf War showed a United States of America at the zenith of its power. In the first opportunity to flex its muscles since the collapse of international communism, it deployed awesome force against its Iraqi enemy. But the victory it won left it with a double-edged sword. It challenged sensitivities in the Islamic world. American soldiers were prepared to take orders only from American commanders. Whatever the broad-based nature of the coalition that fought that war, the common perception was that it was an American army under American command that called all the shots. The contribution of the First Gulf War towards a polarized way of thinking, with radicalized Islam identifying the United States (and its allies) as 'the Great Satan' on the one hand and supplying the West's new need for an identifiable 'enemy' on the other, was patent. A scenario had been set up that would allow a number of new factors to evolve and new hostilities to be fostered.

In a different register altogether, but just as decisive a break with all previous practice and, therefore, able to set its own mark on the dawn of this new era, was the Big Bang of October 1987 that saw the deregulation of financial markets and the creation of a global market. Until then, it's not too much of a caricature to suggest that markets in London had been run on a basis that sometimes resembled an old boys' club. Everybody knew everybody else and a large proportion of deals done were concluded over much-famed three-hour lunches. The Stock Exchange operated over the watchword 'My word is my bond' and Lloyd's of London, showing off in Latin, took *uberrima fides* (trust by the bucketful) as its motto. All business was concluded between the sacred hours of 9am and 5pm. After deregulation, however, there was no longer an opening time or a closing time. It was not only commodities or shares that were traded in this non-stop way. Currencies, too, which had long ceased to be tied to a gold standard, had their value determined in the market place.

George Soros, a Hungarian-born financier, was able to use these conditions to his advantage in 1992 at the time when Britain's place in the Exchange Rate Mechanism was being questioned. His adroit interventions in the market place allowed him to make millions at the expense of sterling. 'Black Wednesday' and all that followed saw a spectacular collapse that left Norman Lamont, the Chancellor of the Exchequer, very exposed to public ridicule. It was a massive blow to John Major's nascent government and has sounded warning bells for the Treasury ever since. Who can doubt that the bruising taken by sterling in 1992 contributed materially to the 'prudence' (or is it ultra-caution?) of Gordon Brown as he dealt with the question of whether sterling should enter the Euro zone?

All this has led to the non-stop trading of currencies in a global market place. Trillions of dollars are constantly in movement and this 'virtual' activity, aided by new technologies, can only be conjectured at by non-specialists. Indeed, as the events that led to the collapse of Enron (and the later extradition of the 'Natwest Three') were to show, some of the activities generated within this new financial order were scarcely comprehensible to those at work in the sector either. All this frenetic activity has undoubtedly exposed even major economies to forces that were previously unimaginable. It has effectively inter-nationalized the worlds of commerce and finance. No economist can now do his sums tidily within one national framework. All their economic models will have to take the most varied and complex factors into account – a direct consequence of the Big Bang of 1987.

If the factors dealt with thus far constitute the main elements of a framework that can fittingly be called a new world order, then no one should doubt that there are many other features that contribute to its overall shape and size. Ongoing and simmering disputes like those in Kashmir, Northern Ireland, Chechnya, the Democratic Republic of the Congo, Darfur and Indonesia make a sorry list. Natural disasters like the 2005 tsunami, the Pakistani earthquake and the flooding of New Orleans in the aftermath of hurricane Katrina remind us of the capacity of nature to create its own agenda and to impose wanton suffering on countless people. Climate change and global warming are likely to have many other such surprises in store in the years to come.

And then, to bring this long decade to an end, there was 9/11. Most people remember where they were that fateful Tuesday. We watched the whole drama unfold. Our work was abandoned. Incredulity mixed with horror filled our souls. We saw the planes hit the World Trade Center buildings in New York. We watched the flames, the people jumping, the billowing smoke, the collapse of the towers. So many people could remember how they had recently stood as tourists on top of them. The news from other incidents in Washington and Pennsylvania soon followed and we knew that this would lead to a crisis of the first order. It would raise issues of a magnitude we could only at that time guess at.

Some of the pictures now associated with that momentous day are ineradicably written on our minds. The vacuous look on the face of President George W. Bush as an aide leaned over him to whisper the news in his ear was just one. He was sitting in front of a group of children at the time. Then there were the billowing clouds of dust and debris, the traumatized crowds running away from downtown Manhattan, the 'disappearance' of Vice-President Dick Cheney, and the arm-waving Palestinians, so many of whom greeted the news with joy and exhilaration. After the images came the words. The 'war against terror', 'the axis of evil', 'we'll flush them out' – all these graphic phrases and others too are part of a new discourse born as a direct consequence of 9/11.

Soon other images were clustering and competing for our attention: the bombing of mountain hideaways in Afghanistan, the features of Osama bin Laden, the tightening of security controls in all sorts of places, the prisoners seized and incarcerated in Guantanamo Bay, the deep-lined anger written on the faces of American politicians.

It was obvious that a mood of palpable fear had spread around the globe. It was equally clear that a great deal of this was feeding a barely hidden and increasingly vociferous mistrust (bordering on hatred) of Muslims. Radical fundamentalists may well have acted in the name of their religion but the unbridled feelings being released were now being directed at Muslims in general. And these feelings were mutual as many in the Muslim world developed a categorical and visceral hatred for the United States and its allies.

Rowan Williams, whose name had only just been announced to the world as the incoming Archbishop of Canterbury, was in New York at the time of the strike on the World Trade Center towers. He penned a little book, a masterpiece of its kind, called *Writing in the Dust*. He offered an immediate theological assessment of the incidents that he'd had such close contact with. Many of us wished that this little book had become the manifesto upon which western politicians had reflected long and hard before rushing in to precipitate action.

Williams was addressing a church meeting in downtown Manhattan, just a few blocks from the twin towers, on that fateful morning. In his very opening remarks he points to the paradox that struck him at once. The passengers in the planes were using their mobile phones to talk to their spouses and families in those desperate last minutes. At the same time, one of the terrorists was communicating to his collaborators how to prepare themselves mentally for the death they had chosen for themselves (and for others). The religious words of the terrorists were being used 'to make a martyr's drama out of a crime'. At the same time, the non-religious words of the victims are full of the content normally carried by religious language – 'the triumph of pointless, gratuitous love, the affirming of faithfulness even when there's nothing to be done or salvaged'. The first little chapter of this remarkable essay is a reminder of a 'frightening contrast'. The terrorists mouth a discourse that is 'murderously spiritual', while their victims, 'compassionately secular', seem full of a profound spirituality. The 9/11 tragedy threw up one example after another of this contrast. But people were too afraid to think, they were in denial and shock. It's a common observation of bereavement that shock and denial soon give way to anger. This was the critical path that we were soon witnessing in the aftermath of 9/11. The American people's emotions were all over the place and their political leaders preyed on this as they formulated their responses to the terrorists' attacks. The establishment of a new Homelands Security agency and the visible presence of highly armed members of the security services offered just some of the evidence of the new mood of the times. It was clear that we had entered a new and fearful moment in our history. Thus the 1990s drew to their conclusion.

This little book has been written against just such a backdrop. It's an attempt to read the signs of our times. A great deal has been written and much more offered at the level of commentary and opinion since the attack on the twin towers. Not all of it has been helpful and much of it is mystifying. We dare to hope that what follows will offer a rational approach to what's happening in the complex world we live in, and that it will serve as a 'discussion starter' or even (who knows?) guidance amid a welter of information and an overflow of passionate feeling.

Much that's come from the world of theology has an apocalyptic note about it. This has sometimes been offered in the guise of a prophetic word, a word of warning which, being interpreted, might go something as follows:

> Thus saith the Lord, a crisis is looming. There may still be time to rescue the planet but you're leaving it late. You must repent of your wrong-doing, change your ways and embrace new priorities. And that right soon. Otherwise you'll see the abomination of desolation in your midst and are likely to be consumed in the incalculable consequences of your own pig-headedness. This generation is eating sour grapes but it will be the teeth of your children and your children's children that will be set on edge.

A dire outlook indeed. Other commentators from a more conservative corner of the world of faith, meanwhile, suggest that we are witnessing the playing out of an end-time scenario. Wars and rumours of war, troubles in the Middle East, the vengeance to be wreaked by God's chosen people on its enemies, will all lead to Armageddon and the consummation of human history. It is the duty of Christian nations to equip (the state of) Israel for its eschatological role.

Another range of responses, sometimes religious but more often secular, attempts to get a handle on this whole complex and sorry mess by making everything one-dimensional. Pacifism is one such approach. It offers an attractive and coherent world-view and allows one to speak with certitude when all around seem to be losing their heads. And who can be against peace? Slightly more nuanced is the application of the theory of the just war.

It's always good to have criteria that have been shaped over time and in the light of experience. But it might be argued that such thinking has never previously had to take into consideration the nature of present-day conflict. The Israeli military historian Martin van Creveld, in his 1986 book *On Future War,* predicted that wars would be communal clashes, involving gangsters, guerrillas and terrorist groups living in and on the community, as much as the disciplined armies of states. 'The new wars', he argued, 'will not obey the dictates of linear, Newtonian time, they will be cyclical and repetitive.' A prophetic word indeed. Or, as the highly decorated British general Rupert Smith put it in his recent book *The Utility of Force,* the industrial force of state armies, with tanks, laser bombs and remote controlled drones, can only be of limited value against guerrillas ands terrorists. Though the armies are capable of a tactical win, by smashing bunkers, bombing villages and 'knocking out' rocket and missile sites, strategic victory is elusive because it requires the changing of hearts and minds. Smith concludes that much of the contest in modern arenas of conflict 'will be outside the state' and will involve a battle 'for sympathy and support in the "information space" of public media of all kinds'.

Taking sides is another relatively straightforward thing to do. A pro-Palestinian (or pro-Israeli) stance in the Middle East, for example, gives someone the possibilities of commitment to a cause and the chance to campaign for 'our side' and, of course, against their opponents. And then there's the United Nations with its respect for the nation states that make up its membership. Here, it's the sovereignty of the state and the inviolability of borders that serve as bedrock for any argument constructed from within the worlds of politics or international law. And many a case has been put forward in this way without a critical questioning of the assumptions underlying the provisions of the United Nations Charter. Are they still fit for their purpose?

We want to argue that there are particular characteristics in play just now that make it necessary to dig as deeply into our imaginations as into our law books or our Bibles. We have to take the pulse of the morning we're living in and offer a diagnosis for healthy and creative ways forward. Of course, it will be necessary to remain true to our fundamental convictions but we will argue that these can sometimes be far more flexible than we might have imagined and, indeed, will need to be if we're to get beyond present positions.

There's no sense in which we can simply apply the teaching of the Bible to our present situation. That would be to dishonour its authority and to misunderstand its status. For all that, we have wanted to look at the way people's thinking develops within the biblical narrative. How did the community of belief in the ancient world respond to changing circumstance? What evidence is there that the Bible, far from being a static text, actually takes its own arguments further, modifies stances previously adumbrated before moving to new ground, ground that offers a different vantage point from which to view familiar events? We don't want to pursue this line of analysis on the basis of material marginal to the biblical narrative. So we've chosen to look at the Exodus and the Council of Jerusalem. You can't get much more central to the biblical story of faith than that! Chapter 2 will look at these two events and show how particularism, ethno-centrism and cultural absolutism, all present within the narrative, give way under the pressure of events and yield a more universal stance. This chapter suggests that the very idea of such a development might open up methodologies and angles of view from which we can learn to look at our contemporary world in a more imaginative way.

The heart of this book lies in the two matching chapters (3 and 4) that follow, each of which sets out six 'case studies'. Thus, side by side, we have sought to illustrate the key thrust of our argument, which might be stated thus:

1 A number of situations of conflict have arisen since the end of the Cold War. On the whole, the mechanisms available to the international community for dealing with conflict are unwieldy. Even localized disputes have taken years to deal with and caused an enormous amount of suffering along the way. We shall examine (Chapter 3) in some detail the recent histories of Bosnia, East Timor, Eritrea, Haiti, Iraq and Rwanda. We might, of course, have lengthened our list to include Chechnya, Sri Lanka and Darfur (among others). But six seemed a fair sample from which to offer some analysis. In all of them, the United Nations has played a role, and the will of the international community has been severely tested. Problem-solving and conflict-resolution have been based almost invariably on respect for

the sovereignty of the state and the inviolability of borders. It might have been better to override such a rigid application of the provisions of the United Nations Charter in Bosnia and Rwanda where it was clear that genocide or crimes against humanity had probably taken place. On the whole, the idea of the sovereignty of the state has proved to be an unquestionable axiom of international law in its approach to situations of conflict.

2 The world order that was shaped in the aftermath of the Second World War was driven by the need to ensure that no such global conflict ever happened again. So the Bretton Woods agreements were set up. The United Nations and its agencies were established. The World Bank, the International Monetary Fund and the International Court of Justice became pillars of the post-war arrangements. State sovereignty, enshrined in the UN Charter, became the cornerstone of UN policy. As the colonial era drew to its close, a time that saw dozens of new nations come into being, this became an even more important consideration.

3 While this picture was emerging and taking shape, other realities were also developing that presented a radical challenge to its assumptions. Across a number of fronts, it was obvious that a new and global order was coming into being. Forces that play a large and determinative part in the daily lives and destinies of the whole human race were moving abroad. *These forces have proved to be no respecters of borders.* They rove the globe with impunity. To illustrate this phenomenon, we examine (Chapter 4) (1) the way international crime has expanded; (2) the way the needs of the environment and the prospect of global warming have begun to impact on governments and peoples in every corner of the planet; (3) the way our financial markets operate at will across the globe; (4) the ease with which disease moves from country to country and continent to continent; (5) the contribution of the internet and information technology to a world wide web of knowledge; and (6) the migrations of people in unprecedented numbers as refugees or internally displaced people or asylum seekers. Again, we trust that six such areas of concern will offer an adequate sample for the purpose of our case. Popular music, tourism and advertising (among other things) could have been added to this list.

The mechanisms for problem-solving or conflict-resolution available to us seem so ill-matched to the realities we all live with in our contemporary world. They were largely brought into being for a world facing the post-1945 realities and were a brilliant and committed response to the needs of the world at that time. And traditional ways of thinking about conflict and the nature of war could properly be employed in a world that still seemed to be connected by 'Newtonian time' to the era that had preceded it. But how should we shape instruments that will be better tuned to the needs of our own times? The question is an urgent one and, in our final chapter (Chapter 5), we'll offer some tentative thoughts by way of a response to this question. Just as there were biblical writers who needed to re-assess the way they'd previously thought about the key events in their 'salvation history', so too it seems necessary for us to do the same.

Rebecca West put things very simply in her classic account of Yugoslavia, *Black Lamb and Grey Falcon*, in which she described Europe hurtling into the Second World War. 'Only part of us is sane,' she wrote,

> only part of us loves pleasure and the longer day of happiness, wants to live to our nineties and die in peace, in a house that we built, that shall shelter those who come after us. The other half of us is nearly mad. It prefers the disagreeable to the agreeable, loves pain and its darker night despair, and wants to die in a catastrophe that will set back life to its beginnings and leave nothing of our house save its blackened foundations.

As we watched the young and idealistic people leave the Manse on that February day in 2003, our hearts grieved for them and for ourselves. At least they were doing something. But was it mere self-deception on their part? Curmudgeonly cynicism on ours? What exactly do we (or can we) do when the world seems to prefer the disagreeable to the agreeable and the nations seem bent on leaving nothing on the face of the planet but blackened foundations?

2

Light to Lighten the Nations

In his ground-breaking book, *The Dignity of Difference,* the Chief Rabbi, Sir Jonathan Sacks, makes a powerful case for tolerance and sensitivity. He argues that the world has for too long been dominated by what he calls 'universalist cultures' whose sway was marked by the extinction of weaker forms of life and the diminution of difference. Local customs and ancient traditions were swept away. Thus, the ancient empires of Greece and Rome, medieval Christianity and Islam, as well as the Enlightenment, imposed themselves with monolithic effect. 'They were to cultural diversity', Sacks argues, 'what industrialization is to biodiversity.'

He isn't blind to the great legacies of these cultures but he regrets the loss of difference that was a consequence of the way they imposed themselves. He goes on to plead for 'a theology of difference'. Unity, he insists, creates diversity and the time has come for people of different groups, different faiths, to make more of an effort to heed and hear each other.

> Any proposed reduction of that diversity through the many forms of fundamentalism that exist today – market, scientific or religious – would result in a diminution of the rich texture of our shared life, a potentially disastrous narrowing of the horizons of possibility.

His plea that, in a global age, it is vital to honour and esteem the different faith and cultural groupings that make up our human family, to give them their proper dignity, is made passionately and with great eloquence and erudition. He makes an incontestable case. And yet there seems to be another side of the coin. However important it is to emphasize the various strands of our diversity, we must surely go on to ask a further question about the kind of world our different groupings want to live in, what kind of social order we need to build to accommodate them and allow them to contribute to the common good. It may well be true, as the Chief Rabbi argues, that unity creates diversity, but an equally compelling case can be made that diversity begs the question of unity. Subsidiarity supposes an overarching solidarity. Can we, while dignifying difference, identify the kind of unity we aspire to? Indeed, can we possibly stop at the level of mere aspiration? We need to make as strong a case as we can, fully aware of the importance of all that makes us different, for the necessity of finding ways in our daily lives of living out the realities of our (human) bio-diversity while at the same time identifying the values and goals that unite us beyond difference. The parts, important as they are, must come together so that they release energies in each other: the product must be more than the sum of those separate parts. This has to do with synergy where groups catalyze each other and bring a greater reality into view. This is more than a matter of mere arithmetic.

We offer this essay as Christians but we shall make no attempt within these pages to look for or identify a theological strand running throughout world events or recent history. We have seen too many church reports where the theological or biblical material has felt 'bolted on' or woven through an otherwise sensible piece. This has left such work open to accusations of special pleading. In contrast, while we shall want to argue, and argue very strongly, that what happens around us takes on new meaning when viewed from the position of faith, it hardly helps us prove our case to prop up our argument with spurious or lazy appeals to Scripture or tradition.

We want here to suggest that Christians will bring their own instincts and understandings, their own angle of view, to the events and phenomena described in later chapters of this book. Not that all Christians will agree in their interpretation of these. Pacifists and those committed to traditional theories of a just war will certainly reach their conclusions according to their own light. Neither of these may accord with the views of those who have a more open or nuanced view of conflict, ready to look for other ways to analyse and understand what they consider to be radical new forms of violence and terror which none of the methodologies or convictions previously adhered to seems able fully to deal with.

With all this in mind, it may be useful to attempt to describe the 'angle of view' from which a Christian might look at contemporary events. In doing so, and in adducing biblical material to help us in this task, we must recognize immediately how difficult (dangerous even) it can be to argue from the Bible to contemporary events. The Bible is, after all, a culturally conditioned collection of writings. We cannot come to it looking for particular answers to particular questions. Those living in biblical times had no knowledge of East Timor or HIV/Aids or the movement of capital in a global market. Nor should we look for cheap answers or false solutions to the problems facing us by turning the Bible into an abstract set of truths unrelated to space or time. It is surely not appropriate that we siphon off what we might call 'timeless truths' into a sort of ethereal realm that has nothing to do with space–time reality in order then, when it suits our purpose, to carry them across from the first century to our own in an attempt to make them 'relevant' to a new and totally unrelated situation.

So how then, if at all, can the Bible be useful to anyone wanting to bring the apparatus of faith to bear on the complexities of twenty-first-century life?

A Welshman in London could easily choose to court the company of his fellow-countrymen and -women and live out his social life as if the rest of the world didn't exist; this would be a life made up of *eisteddfods*, singing festivals, Welsh pubs and chapels, the language of the Bards and carefully chosen and cultivated friendships, all souped up by frequent visits across Offa's Dyke. A similar scenario could be painted for someone with origins in Yorkshire or any other strongly regional part of the country.

Nor is it difficult to imagine a Christian living in Golders Green, a very Jewish part of London, where one's neighbours would be drawn from a wide spectrum of Jewish life. They could be secular or religious, Ashkenazi or Sephardi, Russian, French, German or American – it would be very easy to bury one's head in the sand and keep oneself to oneself, maintaining a dignified sense of difference, mingling only with fellow-Christians. If such a scene were transferred to Whitechapel or Southall, the neighbours would tend to be Muslims or Hindus.

In each case, the proud Welshman or Yorkshirewoman on the one hand, and the convinced Christian on the other, would have lived a less-than-rich life. They'd have played to the lowest common denominator and lost so many opportunities. In the name of affirming difference, they could well have missed out on the stimulus of living on a larger map and enjoying wider cultural and human blessings. And they might also have turned their backs on an obligation to work to create a community where difference is seen not as a fragmenting factor but as the raw material for building a peaceful world.

The congregation of Wesley's Chapel on London's City Road brings together people from three dozen different national backgrounds. Sunday by Sunday, the whole world is present in microcosm. They bring their different languages, their varied cultures and ethnicities into a congregational life that is staggeringly rich and varied. The different strands of fellowship present are honoured and every effort is made to cherish those whose lives have been shaped and influenced by countries and cultures ranging from Fiji to Finland, Argentina to Zimbabwe, the United Kingdom to the United States of America. But the greatest challenge faced by such a multicultural congregation flows from the fact that, without denying the wealth of its diversity, regular glimpses are gained of a reality beyond difference, a realm of experience where it is possible to grasp at the fact of a common humanity to which all human beings belong fully and equally and without distinction. Transcending difference then becomes the watchword. In affirming all those characteristics that distinguish people from one another and confer on each his/her identity, it is entirely appropriate to want to rejoice in them, share them, enrich each other through them; but it also seems a logical next step to want to bring them to a greater cause. For if people content themselves with gathering clannishly within their own cultural, ethnic, gender or generational groupings, without identifying (and committing themselves to) realities that lie beyond their differences, then fragmentation rather than community-building will become the order of the day. Self-ghettoization cannot be enough.

There are two highly significant moments in the Bible, one in each Testament, when a process of change culminates in profound insight about the nature of human society and offers a basis for building a different kind of future. Each of these is at the very heart of the biblical narrative. They are foundational events in the formation respectively of the nation of Israel and the Christian Church. They offer an important key to understanding both the nature of Scripture and also the elements of its world-view. It is not part of our case to suggest or imply that events in the centuries before Christ or in the first generation of the Christian Church can simply be transferred to our contemporary world. These insights are offered with a somewhat different object in mind. In each of them, the participants in a particular historical event are required to revise previously held convictions and are challenged to face the future in the light of new understandings of previously cherished principles. And, in each case, the movement is away from an exclusive viewpoint to something altogether more inclusive, from the particular to the universal.

The Exodus

The Exodus is central to any understanding of the theology of the Old Testament. This was an event that gave identity to a people, one to which they referred again and again. And it also offered a lasting paradigm to which many 'liberation movements' across the ages could appeal as they set out their case and struggled for their freedom. Bondage in the house of Egypt, the leadership of Moses, his readiness to insist to the wicked Pharaoh that he should 'let my people go', the plagues, the Passover, the parting of the Red Sea, the wilderness years, the ten commandments, the arrival on 'the verge of Jordan', the death of Moses and the triumphal entry into the Promised Land are the main elements of a story that was remembered down the centuries. No one can seriously doubt its fundamental importance in establishing a world-view that was repeated generation after generation in the liturgical life of the Jewish people. But, within Scripture itself, there are varying views of this foundational event which suggest a readiness to interpret even material of such overarching importance in the light of historical experience.

Most scholars accept that the Pentateuch brings together at least four literary sources. The editorial shape of the Pentateuch has been dominated by the earliest of these ('the Jahwist') and by the latest (the 'priestly' source). The first of these, drawing on material already centuries old, was brought together at some time during the tenth century BC at a time when Israel was experiencing relative peace in a land of its own and enjoying status among the nations under the leadership of David and Solomon. It was at this period, the time of the 'united monarchy', that editors set about writing the nation's history in order to show how Israel had come to this golden age. Everything flowed from the plan and fidelity of a promise-making God. Bearing this in mind, the Exodus could readily be seen as a continuation of the story of promise begun in the book of Genesis and completed when Israel reached the Promised Land as recorded in the book of Numbers.

The optimistic historiography of the Jahwist was, of course, challenged by later events. The division of the kingdom and especially the loss of its northern part to the Assyrians in the eighth century seemed at odds with the triumphalism of this earlier account. The discovery of the book of Deuteronomy in 621 BC, during the reign of King Josiah, offered a radical re-appraisal of sacred history. One of the main thrusts of Deuteronomy was to address the perceived weakening of the national religious life. The perception had grown that the practice of worshipping at the various shrines scattered over the land, with all the dangers of syncretism attendant upon such practice, needed to be 'corrected'. One of the main thrusts of the book is the command to centralize the cult in the Jerusalem temple. The people are criticized for having outgrown the old ordinances of Israel. These are given great emphasis and even toughened up. Indeed, there is what one scholar (Gerhard von Rad) has described as 'a warlike spirit' in evidence throughout the book. This is nowhere more obvious than in the gruesome reminder that the first generation of those who crossed the Jordan were commanded to exterminate the populations already living in the land – the Hittites, the Girgashites, the Amorites, the Canaanites, the Perizzites, the Hivites and the Jebusites. They should be shown no mercy and it would be an offence to allow any assimilation with them. This harsh line, what our commentator calls 'militant piety', is one way of dealing with decadence, decline and military defeat. As we shall see presently, it isn't the only one on display.

The last of the editorial traditions woven into the Pentateuchal narrative emanated from sixth-century priestly circles. It was written during the Babylonian Exile for a generation that had lost its identity as a politically independent people. It sought to re-interpret the story of the Exodus for those who were without land, nation or king. The priestly tradition viewed the Exodus as a new and definite act of divine self-revelation and as a means for both Israel and Egypt to know Yahweh. Yahweh's main intention in bringing the people out of bondage was that he might dwell among them. Israel should, according to this tradition, think of itself as a religious congregation rather than a political entity, a people made holy by Yahweh's tabernacling presence and whose primary link with God was the cult.

These different historiographies, all to be found within the Pentateuch, show a readiness to shape the interpretation of events to suit either the new facts of history or the ideological requirements of historians. When we turn elsewhere in the Old Testament, we find this process continuing. A particularly vivid re-interpretation of the Exodus is offered by the prophet we've come to know as 'Second Isaiah', who dates from the sixth century BC. His writings (mainly to be found in chapters 40—55 of the canonical book of Isaiah) are a direct response to the conquest of Judah in 586 BC by the Babylonians and the subsequent exile of its people.

How could God have allowed his chosen people to undergo such humiliation? What point now in clinging to a 'triumphalist' interpretation of the Exodus? The people that once languished in Egyptian bondage now find themselves in Babylonian exile. Their pride and readiness to turn their backs on the covenant have manifested themselves again and again. Now, it seems, the wheel has to be re-invented. The people have to be motivated to make the long trek home all over again. A new Exodus must be envisaged.

The prophet reworks the material explicitly and with radical intent. Once again, in his scheme of things, 'the wilderness', far from representing the ultimate danger and annihilation of life, now actually becomes the precondition for God's demonstration of his unique special power and faithfulness. It will prove to be the place of the divine revelation as once happened at Sinai. 'In the wilderness prepare the way of the Lord,' the prophet cries,

> make straight in the desert a highway for our God. Every valley shall be lifted up, and every mountain and hill be made low; the uneven ground shall become level, and the rough places a plain. Then the glory of the Lord shall be revealed, and all people shall see it together, for the mouth of the Lord has spoken. (Isa. 40.3–5)

The people now in exile are every bit as 'afflicted, wretched and poor' as they were so many centuries earlier in Egypt. And God wishes to offer a new and renewing beginning, to start all over again.

> Thus says the Lord, who makes a way in the sea, a path in the mighty waters, who brings out chariot and horse, army and warrior; they lie down, they cannot rise, they are extinguished, quenched like a wick: 'Do not remember the former things, or consider the things of old. I am about to do a new thing; now it springs forth, do you not perceive it? I will make a way in the wilderness and rivers in the desert. The wild animals will honour me, the jackals and the ostriches; for I give water in the wilderness, rivers in the desert, to give drink to my chosen people, the people whom I formed for myself.' (Isa. 43.16–21)

In the prophet's narrative, the Exodus is not quoted as an event concluded in the past: rather, it is seen as profoundly characteristic and continuously constitutive of his nature (the participle *making a way* conveys this sense of an ongoing activity). This is something that goes on happening, age after age. Whereas the first Exodus was marked by the corpses of the Egyptians who were extinguished like a wick, the new Exodus is actually applauded even by 'jackals and ostriches'. This new Exodus transforms the world of nations. Its central, theological figure is drawn in ideal terms in the four Songs of the Suffering Servant of God (Isa. 42.1-4, 5-9; 49.1-6, 7-9; 50.4-9, 10-11; 52.13—53.12).

The first Exodus was the event that showed God's triumph in combating primal chaos ('Was it not you who cut Rahab in pieces, who pierced the dragon?'). Once more, we are to understand his readiness to take up this struggle, but now he intends to give his unlimited power a new direction. He wants to wean Israel away from all ideas of a strong God who destroys the enemy; he wants Israel to discover that he is a loving God who wants to bestow new life, first and foremost to Israel itself:

> I, I am he who comforts you; why then are you afraid of a mere mortal who must die . . . ? The oppressed shall speedily be released; they shall not die and go down to the Pit, neither shall they lack bread. For I am the Lord your God . . . and . . . you are my people. (Isa. 51.12-16)

The covenant promise, for all the lapses that have occurred on Israel's side, holds good.

Jerusalem will become the place where God chooses to reveal his new purposes; it will be the new Sinai. If God has been understood by his people as a God of war, he will now disclose himself as a caring Shepherd of his people. His manifesto can be summed up in the word *shalom* (Isa. 52.7). The new Exodus will be undertaken by a people setting out to acknowledge the kingly reign of this caring God who wishes to install an era of peace. They will not leave their exile in the same way as their forbears left Egypt, as if leaving a prison camp or a slave compound. This will not be a procession that resembles the flight of the remnants of a defeated army. This will be a peaceful and solemn affair.

> Depart, depart, go out from there! Touch no unclean thing; go out from the midst of it, purify yourselves, you who carry the vessels of the Lord. For you shall not go out in haste, and you shall not go in flight; for the Lord will go before you, and the God of Israel will be your rearguard. (Isa. 52.11–12)

A shepherd at the head has to lead the way; one who brings up the rear keeps the animals together. The contrast could hardly be clearer. God the Shepherd replaces God the warrior who figures so strongly in the first Exodus.

If God shows himself first to Israel, it is with a far wider purpose in mind. The task for which he has prepared his people through the catastrophe of exile, and through Israel's political powerlessness in post-exilic times, is that they should give an example to the nations of the justice and righteousness of God (Isa. 42.1, 4). 'Listen to me, my people, and give heed to me, my nation; for a teaching will go out from me, and my justice for a light to the peoples' (Isa. 51.4). The role played by 'the nations' in this vision of God's plan for his people becomes the major feature, the culmination of the prophet's proclamation.

The place taken by Sinai in the priestly document is occupied by Jerusalem in Isaiah's thinking. 'The nations shall see your vindication,' he writes, 'and all the kings your glory' (Isa. 62.2). This rethinking of the role of the nations leads to a worldwide policy of peace. Different from the first Exodus is the fact that at the centre there no longer stands the cult but the social and political ethos. In a third-century redaction of the whole book of Isaiah, a process that modified earlier material and gave us the biblical book as it now stands, this thinking is taken even further.

> Then the moon will be abashed, and the sun ashamed; for the Lord of hosts will reign on Mount Zion and in Jerusalem, and before his elders he will manifest his glory . . . On this mountain the Lord of Hosts will make for all peoples a feast of rich food, a feast of

well-matured wines . . . And he will destroy on this mountain the shroud that is cast over all peoples, the sheet that is spread over all nations; he will swallow up death for ever. Then the Lord God will wipe away the tears from all faces, and the disgrace of his people he will take away from all the earth, for the Lord has spoken. (Isa. 24.23; 25.6–8)

A new Moses will be sent to bring about the realization of this vision. No longer will Israel's two major enemies, Egypt and Assyria, be afflicted by plagues, nor will God visit them with desolation and death as in the first Exodus. Now 'The Lord will strike Egypt, striking and healing; they will return to the Lord, and he will listen to their supplications and heal them' (Isa. 19.22). Then Egypt and Assyria will join with Israel, God's possession, and become one 'people of God' as a result of Israel's lived witness: 'On that day Israel will be the third with Egypt and Assyria, a blessing in the midst of the earth' (Isa. 19.24).

And so what began as a tale of liberation from the Egyptian house of bondage looks towards the abolition of all houses of bondage. And this readiness to recognize that Israel's doctrine of 'manifest destiny' needed to be re-examined in the light of history and moved from its particularist stance towards something more all-embracing is one that offers important methodological material for looking at situations of conflict at any time in history. The question will always be how nations and faiths move beyond a narrowly defined understanding of their own needs and interests, how to appropriate the understanding that the common good represents the true wealth of the nations.

The Council of Jerusalem

This dynamic is evident in the way the earliest Christians reinterpreted the death of Jesus. What had seemed to be the defeat and death of Jesus was now experienced as God's triumphant restoration and exaltation of the crucified Messiah. The implications of the presence of Jesus with and among the infant churches, according to Luke, begins with the giving of the Spirit to all the apostles at Pentecost.

The Spirit is then shared with Jewish believers gathered in Jerusalem and representing all the nations. What this meant for the future had to be worked out by the earliest followers of Jesus in their experience, and thought out by careful reflection on earlier scriptural writing. What in the light of these new events, was the place of Jesus in the purposes of God? How in these new circumstances were the apostles and the churches they founded to be faithful to the message of Jesus? What was God's purpose not only for Jerusalem but for all the nations of the world?

In the year AD 50 a Council was called in Jerusalem, the very first gathering of Christians from around the Mediterranean world. They had urgent business to attend to. In a single generation since the death of Christ, his cause had won followers in many scattered cities and provinces in the Roman Empire. And the most important, and potentially critical, feature of this expansion was that the cause was breaking out from an original Semitic matrix as more and more Gentiles declared for this new faith.

This raised difficulties in the realm of language. How could ideas and understandings that had been formed in an Aramaic-speaking context (and in the tiny province of Judea) be explained in the Greek or Latin languages then current in the ancient world? And how were those Jews who'd seen Jesus as the Messiah, the fulfilment of their people's ancient hopes and dreams, to relate to these new converts who came from an entirely different thought world? One way might have been to demand that Gentiles become Jews, accepting the disciplines of Judaism. To do this, they would have had to accept circumcision as a rite of passage and a lifestyle based on some very demanding food regulations. As important as all this was the theological question: how could people from such different social, cultural, political and religious backgrounds come to a mind about God's self-disclosure in the person of Jesus Christ? How would such an understanding be framed in a way that would satisfy the needs of such a diverse community of faith?

This was the Church's first experience of multiculturalism. It was a problem that was not going to go away. For four centuries it preoccupied the Fathers of the Church. It was not only the question of finding an accommodation to satisfy both Jewish and Gentile members of the community that needed to be addressed with urgency. So too did the linguistic and philosophical differences in such diverse places as Antioch, Alexandria, Constantinople and Rome. The attempt to harmonize these taxed the minds of some of the best thinkers the world has ever known and began a process that led to the formulation of the Nicene Creed at the Council of Chalcedon in AD 451. Even that didn't resolve the whole matter. Nestorians and Arians were excluded by this process and the Coptic churches of the Arabian peninsula and of Egypt and Ethiopia, as well as the Goths and Visigoths and Vandals who were about to sweep through Central Europe, continued to raise fundamental questions of meaning into the centuries beyond.

This process began at the Council of Jerusalem. It had become clear that the message being preached by Jewish followers of Christ was capable of winning a response in the Gentile world. The part played by the apostle Paul in the transmission of the Christian message is key to this – the erstwhile zealous Jew became 'apostle to the Gentiles'. But the role played by Peter seems to be at least on a par with this. The road that took him (Acts 10) from Joppa to Caesarea matches Paul's from Jerusalem to Damascus. His readiness to sit and eat with Cornelius, a Roman soldier, sharpened the questions that needed to be faced and earned him a great deal of criticism from conservative Jews.

The success of the missionary journey undertaken by Paul and Barnabas (Acts 13 and 14) brought on a crisis that could no longer be shelved. Gentiles heard the message 'and were glad and glorified God'. Conservative Jews were 'filled with jealousy' and stirred up opposition. The missionary tour raised fundamental questions about the unity of the Christian community in a multicultural context. The most natural place to address this agenda was Jerusalem. The 'parties' could be expected to argue their case with passion.

The Pharisees were zealous for the law. Paul and his companions had come to see that the strict requirements of traditional Judaism needed to be re-interpreted in the light of recent experience. Gentiles could not (and should not) be expected to keep every detail of the law, they argued.

When the Council began its deliberations, Paul's enthusiasm could easily be discounted. He was too full of himself and his recent exploits. The interventions of Peter and James (the brother of Jesus), on the other hand, would have been eagerly awaited. They were the acknowledged leaders of Jewish Christians in the diaspora and Jerusalem respectively and the 'circumcision party', those seeking to maintain a traditional (fundamentalist) line for new converts, would have wanted them to speak out clearly on the issues.

Peter must have been a great disappointment to them. He'd clearly been affected by his recent experience in Caesarea. He could make no distinction between Gentile and Jewish believers, he declared, and it seemed obvious to him that God had given the Holy Spirit to both groups. This was quite enough for Peter. There seemed no adequate reason in his mind for requiring Gentile believers to carry any further burden. God had already done everything that needed to be done. To demand more would be a work of supererogation and tantamount to making trial of God. Salvation, Peter concluded, would be through grace rather than through circumcision.

The last word fell to James. No one could doubt his authority. He was, after all, the brother of Jesus and was the undisputed leader of the Christian community in Jerusalem. He'd have been very aware of the murmurings and fulminations of the strict Jews who surrounded him in the mother church. He must, therefore, have taken the wind out of their sails by agreeing with Peter's argument and, further, by going on to underpin that argument with an appeal to Scripture. It's worth pausing over the quotation (Amos 9.11f.) introduced by James at this point since a great deal depends on it. There were two versions of the Jewish Scriptures in circulation at this time. One, the Masoretic Text, offered a traditional Hebrew version. The other, the Septuagint, was a translation of the Masoretic Text into Greek. This had only been done in recent times and there were variations between it and the Hebrew original. And one such variation was used by James in his address to the Council of Jerusalem.

The quotation begins with words that are identical in both versions before it splits radically into two contrasting visions of Israel's role in God's plan:

> After this I shall return and I shall rebuild the tent of David which has fallen and I shall rebuild the ruins of it and I shall set it straight

that they [Israel] may possess the remnant of Edom and all the nations that are called by my name. (Masoretic Text)	that the rest of men may seek the Lord and all the nations on whom my name has been called. (Septuagint)

It's the words of the Septuagint that are put into the mouth of James, a version that takes a view of Israel's vocation in universal (rather than particular) terms. Indeed, the translators and editors of the Septuagint are moving in the same general direction as the later re-interpretations of the Exodus referred to above.

The Council came up with an agreement aimed at uniting Jewish and Gentile Christians. This included dropping the insistence on circumcision for Gentile believers. This was a very significant concession since it abandoned a practice whose origins lay with Abraham. Not everyone accepted this condition at once. Paul had to argue his case furiously again and again (as recorded in his correspondence to the Galatians, Corinthians and Romans). Nor did Paul himself apply this new decision in an even manner. He circumcised Timothy, for example (Acts 16.3), but not Titus (Gal. 2.3).

From the Gentile side an accommodation was reached in respect of the food laws. But it is noteworthy for all who seek to unblock situations where there are conflicting interests that circumcision, so firmly attested by Scripture and the Tradition, ceased to be a requirement for those seeking to follow in the Way. It was quite simply laid on one side and abandoned. With this agreement, the road to evangelizing the whole world now lay open.

Some points to consider

The overriding reason for concentrating on these two scriptural events is quite simple. They have paradigmatic status, they show their respective communities of faith at crucial junctures in their development. The need for change is paramount – historical circumstance has driven people into situations where change cannot be avoided. There are those who resist the very idea of change. In the Old Testament, a priestly caste sought to stabilize a situation of change by battening down the hatches, centralizing religion in the capital city, and resorting to militant piety in order to extirpate loose devotional practices from the national life. Another voice, also ultra-conservative, suggests the redefinition of the Exodus community in cultic rather than political terms. In the New Testament, despite the alarming and heady prospects of a huge expansion in the community of faith, there were those who insisted that nothing of the sort should be allowed to happen if it meant letting go of time-honoured ways of doing things. The cautious will always be found among us.

Alongside these points of view can be found another, altogether different one. Change should be faced and embraced. Revered ways of seeing and doing things might have to give way to new (and renewing) courses of action. The way history is written will have to be looked at. Living within a self-imposed ghetto is just not on. A deal has to be struck if things are to move forward. This smacks of compromise and loss of autonomy to some but it needn't amount to the selling of one's soul. It's more a matter of discerning God's will and being prepared to let go of a cherished status quo.

We began this chapter by mentioning Jonathan Sacks' book *The Dignity of Difference* and suggesting that, alongside difference, we had always to keep a larger picture in mind. The Chief Rabbi knows as well as anyone that there will always be a tension between the legitimate and precious characteristics of groups, races, tribes and nations on the one hand and the need to build community relations and a global order on the other. And he himself understands fully that the dignity of difference must always fit in alongside the need to transcend difference for the common good. He understands it and has committed himself to the wider view in his own writing. 'God is only partially comprehended by any faith,' he writes, 'he is my God but also your God. He is on my side but also on your side. He exists not only in my faith but also in yours.' This is a remarkable sentiment from a religious leader. And it can be matched by others.

> God is universal, religions are particular. Religion is the translation of God into a particular language and thus into the life of a group, a nation, a community of faith. In the course of history, God has spoken to mankind in many languages: through Judaism to Jews, Christianity to Christians, Islam to Muslims. Only such a God is truly transcendental – greater not only than the natural universe but also than the spiritual universe articulated in any single faith, any specific language of human sensibility . . . Only such a world view could reconcile the particularity of cultures with the universality of the human condition.

These sentiments, so clearly and admirably expressed, did not please those of a more conservative bent within the United Synagogue. They led to a profound struggle that resulted in Dr Sacks having to rewrite parts of his book. The words quoted above (and many others of a similar nature) were among the passages eliminated in the book's second edition. There will always be those who want to stay in the womb, safe from contact with a wider world, insistent on keeping things as they have always been. And there will be others who are ready to be radical and pragmatic, capable of working out those compromises needed to advance the cause of the unity of the human family.

The same tension experienced by the Chief Rabbi is clearly present in Holy Scripture. And it underlies all efforts in our contemporary world to re-interpret history in the light of current events and to brace ourselves for possible radical new points of departure that will affirm the particularity of cultures within the universality of the human condition.

3

Why Do the Nations Rage?

It's time to turn our attention to six situations of conflict that boiled over during the 1990s. They present a wide variety of factors but, key among them, a towering inability on the part of the international community to respond quickly or effectively. Consequently, large numbers of casualties, mainly among civilian populations, ensued. The United Nations is a consistent player in all these arenas and its limitations are clearly on view. But the role of major powers begs many questions too – the United Kingdom, the United States, France, Belgium, Australia and the Vatican become complicit too often in these crises. Indeed, they are sometimes their progenitors.

Again and again, the inviolability of borders and the refusal to intervene in the affairs of sovereign states are implicit in efforts to resolve conflict. But the sale (or gift) of arms, the presence of occupying forces seeking to claim a neighbour's territory, the greed for rare resources like oil and gas, the obvious disregard for international codes of behaviour on such matters as genocide, ethnic cleansing and crimes against humanity – all these make the treatment of borders as sacrosanct and absolute appear problematical. The need to develop a different way of looking at the way the world's peoples relate to each other will become patent as we look, even cursorily, at the six 'case studies' that follow.

1 Bosnia

In the summer of 1993, Susan Sontag staged a performance of Samuel Beckett's play *Waiting for Godot*. Once again, as it had done so many times since its first performance in the early 1950s, it sounded its familiar themes of hope and despair, the meaning of life, the meaning of suffering, the stature of waiting. In so many ways, this piece of literature seemed to capture the very essence of the century that gave it birth. Nowhere did it find greater resonance than in the setting chosen for it by Sontag.

It was to the beautiful city of Sarajevo that she travelled to put on the first act of this play, the city that had witnessed the killing of Archduke Franz Ferdinand, heir to the Habsburg throne, in June 1914, an event that led Austria-Hungary to declare war on Serbia and, soon, to the unleashing of the senseless brutalities of the First World War. In one sense, the twentieth century began on that summer's day in Sarajevo. Now, almost 80 years later, Sarajevo was once again in trouble. It was a city under siege. For over a year Serbian heavy artillery, placed commandingly in the hills that encircle the city, had relentlessly pounded its streets and meeting places, its places of worship and its homes. The siege was to last some four years while a saddened world seemed able to do no more than look on. This city's beauty was not limited to its geographical setting or its rich architecture; it flowed also from its population. For here, Jews and Muslims and Christians (both Catholic and Orthodox) had long lived together in peace. Sarajevo, more than any other city, had held out the hope that people can live with diversity and thrive on it. This was in many ways the fulfilment of the Enlightenment dream.

Such hopes were shattered by the long siege. The whole city was reduced to rubble and its population divided against itself. No wonder the bleak hinterland of Beckett's play resonated so profoundly in such a situation. As Sontag herself put it:

There were two performances a day, one at 2.00pm and the other at 4.00pm. In Sarajevo there are only matinees; hardly anybody goes out after dark. Many people were turned away. It was at the 2.00pm performance on 18 August, during the long tragic silence of Vladimir and Estragon which follows the messenger's announcement that Mr Godot isn't coming today, but will surely come tomorrow, that my eyes began to sting with tears. Others were crying too. No one in the audience made a sound. The only sounds were coming from outside the theatre; a UN armoured personnel carrier thundering down the street and the crack of sniper fire.

If Sarajevo encapsulated the deep tragedy that was afflicting the Balkans at that time, so too did Srebrenica. This was one of the 'safe areas' designated by the United Nations in 1993 to protect the civilian population in exchange for a ceasefire and the disarming of Bosnian Muslim units. The plan was never developed or enforced but many civilians who might otherwise have fled the town stayed.

Srebrenica's security was being provided by a Dutch battalion that had been seconded to the UN operation. They were inadequately armed and their mandate proved wrong for the conditions that faced them. Early in 1995 General Ratko Mladic, leader of the Bosnian Serbs, began encroaching on the safe area. He justified his actions by alleging that he was simply retaliating for raids by Bosnian Muslim groups under the command of Naser Osric. When Osric was recalled to Sarajevo for consultations in the spring of 1995, Mladic acted. He cut off food and supplies to Srebrenica, including fuel for the Dutch troops. The UN commanders decided that sustaining the safe areas was no longer tenable.

By July, the overcrowded safe area of Srebrenica had fallen to the Bosnian Serb forces. Forty thousand people were deported; 7,500 men and boys were massacred. There was mass rape and wholesale confusion. As Mladic approached the town, many thousands fled towards the headquarters of the Dutch troops, having been given an assurance that the UN had authorized airstrikes to protect them. These failed to materialize and, once the Serbs had taken the Dutch emplacement, they began to 'evacuate' it. They took away all the boys and men into the nearby woods where they were summarily executed. Over a decade after that atrocity, Mladic and his political master Radovan Karadzic, though wanted to face trial for crimes against humanity, remained at large. Srebrenica seared the conscience of the international community. The world looked on as mass slaughter, the contravention of basic human rights, ethnic cleansing and other war crimes were committed so flagrantly. And the United Nations found itself at every step outwitted by its opponents and ill equipped for the role in which it was cast.

The origins of this strife are deep and complex. Bosnia-Herzegovina is an ancient country which, despite being absorbed within the Ottoman Empire for centuries, never lost its identity. In all of this it is exactly like Serbia, its neighbour. It has precisely as much right to separate existence as Serbia or Croatia. The borders it enjoyed at the beginning of 1992 were not, as Serb propaganda claimed, modern administrative arrangements, established by Tito to Serbia's detriment. Bosnia's borders were virtually unchanged throughout the twentieth century and most of them go back far further. In particular the border along the Drina river dividing Bosnia from Serbia is one of the oldest in Europe, going back over a thousand years. Serbia and the Orthodox world have never occupied land west of that line. In the Middle Ages Bosnia had kings of its own. They were Catholic not Orthodox in religion and Bosnia's links were always closer with Croatia than with Serbia. Nevertheless it was a border area between Latin West and Orthodox East and its Christian inhabitants were probably always divided between the two, depending upon which monastery they were nearest.

Some of Bosnia's population had become Muslim already before the Turkish conquest in the fifteenth century. In the sixteenth and seventeenth centuries, the Muslim authorities in Bosnia favoured the Orthodox at the expense of the Catholics (because their principal foreign enemies, such as Venice and Austria, were Roman Catholic). In consequence, the Orthodox Church grew under the Turks while the Roman Catholic Church declined. From the nineteenth century, the Orthodox in Bosnia came to call themselves Serbs, the Roman Catholics Croats. This owed much to the modern establishment of the Patriarchate of Belgrade and the consequent dependence of Orthodox Christians in Bosnia upon Belgrade, a relationship that had not previously existed. Very few of the Muslim population are of Turkish descent. The three religious groups within Bosnia share an identical

Bosnian ethnic background. Before the atrocities of the early 1990s, it was estimated that 44 per cent of the population was Muslim, 31 per cent Serb and 16 per cent Croat. The relations between them were almost always exceptionally tolerant and friendly. The profound Christian–Muslim antagonism engendered in Serbian history was strikingly absent within Bosnia. The tendency of Bosnian Catholics to identify with Croatia was probably in part a reaction on their part to the 'Serbianization' of their Orthodox neighbours.

From the mid-nineteenth century Serbs, who now had a small independent state of their own, wished to extend it across all southern Slavic lands which were at that time still ruled either by the Ottoman or by the Austrian Empire. The 'Greater Serbia' myth arose at that time. Bosnia had been a largely self-governing province of the Turkish Empire until, in the 1870s, it was taken over by the Austrians. Serb nationalists believed that, following the expulsion of the Turks and Austrians, Bosnia should be handed over to them. It was perhaps an understandable piece of nationalist arrogance in the circumstances of the late nineteenth century, but it was never justified as Bosnia had always been a deeply different society from Serbia. For all that, Bosnians accepted the arrangement set out in the Treaty of Versailles establishing the new state of Yugoslavia as an extension of Serbia. This at once resulted in severe anti-Muslim policies pursued by the Belgrade government, however, both in Bosnia and in Kosovo. There were major massacres by Serbs of Muslims in Kosovo in 1921. There was also a policy of enforced settlement of Serbs in Bosnia in the following years.

Tito (himself a Croat) ruled Yugoslavia after the Second World War in an even-handed way as regards the relationships between its many different groups. This was very different both from the Serb domination of the inter-war years and the violent anti-Serb reaction of the Ustase (fascist) Croat government during the war. Once he died, however, Serb dominance was resumed. This was made possible by the fact that they formed the most numerous single group and controlled the capital as well as, to a very large extent, the army. During the 1980s, Slobodan Milosevic came to power just as an increasingly virulent nationalist revival was developing in Serbia. In the period following the collapse of communism, he cleverly switched his allegiances in order to build and consolidate a power base in Serbian nationalism.

When Slovenia and Croatia were violently attacked by the Serb-controlled federal army in the summer of 1991, they immediately sought to withdraw from the former Yugoslavia. The European Community and the United Nations recognized their independence early in 1992. Bosnia was slower to act but, when offered the same possibility, moved to a referendum that gave a vote of over 60 per cent in favour of independence. The proposed government for Bosnia included members of all its ethnic and religious groupings. It has never resembled in any way or to any degree a Muslim fundamentalist state. Yet that was the claim made by the Serbian nationalists and the excuse used by Radovan Karadzic, not himself a Bosnian, to stir up the Bosnian Serbs and to seek the destruction of the country. He was backed in his efforts by the heavy artillery and the planes of Serbia.

Karadzic and his 'Chetniks' set about 'cleansing' Bosnia. He ordered the removal of all non-Serb populations from the places they and their families had inhabited for centuries. His forces stopped short at nothing. The atrocities included the rape and mutilation of women and children and there were mass killings. As soon as an area was crushed, it was cleansed of all signs of non-Serb identity. Catholic churches and mosques were totally destroyed, Muslim tombstones were removed, as the 'Serbianization' of Bosnia took place.

Britain held the presidency of the European Community during the most critical period in the build-up of these atrocities and called a conference in London to address the issues arising from them. The agreements reached were honourable enough but never implemented. Indeed, Britain always dragged its heels. And how! Douglas Hurd opposed attempts to lift the arms embargo, an act that would have allowed the Bosnians to defend themselves against the immensely powerful Serbian army. 'We don't want a level killing field,' he declared, a remark that led one critic to observe that that would at least be better than an un-level killing field. There was a major rift with the Americans (who wanted to arm the Bosnians) and at one stage Malcolm Rifkind, who'd never been a combatant in any conflict, lost his cool with Senator Bob Dole. 'You Americans don't know the horrors of war,' he shouted at a man who'd lost an arm in World War II. Senator John McCain came close to slapping Rifkind at one meeting. At the height of the conflict, Britain effectively closed its borders to Bosnian refugees. 'The civilians have an effect on the combatants,' Hurd explained; 'their interests put pressure on the warring factions to treat for peace.' This disgraceful announcement can only mean that Hurd was denying sanctuary to the victims of the Serbs (and of his own diplomacy) so that he could use their misery to force the Bosnians to cut a deal with the ethnic cleansers.

Soon a discourse had been developed whereby the Bosnian government, despite being thoroughly secular, was repeatedly referred to as 'the Muslims'. Foreign Office mandarins constantly spoke of Bosnian leaders as belonging to one 'warring faction' or another. This was a land filled, so the narrative went, with 'ancient hatreds'. MI6 put out the story that the Bosnians were massacring themselves! The Bosnian war became a strange beast, a perpetratorless crime in which all were victims and all more or less equally guilty. General Sir Michael Rose, who became an armchair guru beloved of the media in subsequent conflicts, even found a good word for the butcher of Srebrenica, General Ratko Mladic, who, he felt, 'generally kept his word'. At one stage, Rose put the demands for a military intervention down to 'the powerful Jewish lobby behind the Bosnian state'. This same officer, attending a performance of Mozart's *Requiem* in Sarajevo, wondered if Alija Izetbegovic, the cultured Bosnian President, could possibly understand 'the Christian sentiment behind the words and music'. Even the media, generally against intervention and not very sensitive to the nuances of the situation, thrashed around in palpable ignorance. Kirsty Wark described a Catholic Croat Bosnian spokesperson as a 'Muslim' on *Newsnight* and ignored him when he protested that he was no such thing. And the BBC's Misha Glenny put the atrocities down to 'ancient irrational beliefs' that drove all parties in the Balkans into cycles of insane slaughter. Douglas Hurd accused the Americans of wanting to recolonize the Balkans, while the Vance-Owen plan to divide Bosnia into enclaves according to ethnicity was a real attempt to 'Balkanize' the Balkans (a plan that one wit described as 'a cartographer's dream and an administrator's nightmare'). Everything was a mess.

In the end, of course, common sense prevailed. After a period of what one analyst calls the 'humanitarianization' of the war, a time when armed forces were sent into Bosnia to protect those taking aid and relief supplies (but with no mandate to engage in military action), it became more and more inevitable that Slobodan Milosovic's bluff should be called. Croatians and Bosnians proved far more ready to play their part than had been feared and they did so without causing a Third World War (an apocalyptic scenario that had been projected by more than one expert). The Serbs were bombed, they folded under pressure and were soon engaged in negotiations for peace. The 1995 Dayton accords, while still dividing Bosnia along ethnic lines, did allow some kind of resolution to the dispute. A United Nations force was deployed to oversee its implementation and, despite the repeated warnings that their presence would not be tolerated, was able to maintain a presence and achieve its purpose.

It remains a reproach on the international community (*pace* Douglas Hurd who at one point exclaimed, echoing a famous utterance made by Margaret Thatcher, 'There is no such thing as the "international community"') that it took so much suffering, such palpable crimes against humanity conducted on a large scale and with little attempt to hide them, before action was finally taken. And we must hold our own government principally to account. Bosnia should remain a reproach on the conscience of all those who showed such an absence of imagination, awareness and political will to address its needs. On this one, at least, the Americans were right.

2 East Timor

East Timor was another accident (and victim) of European colonialism. The fault lines that were to produce so much dreadful suffering were the direct creation of imperial greed and the careless resolution of distant skirmishes. The island of Timor was divided between the Dutch and the Portuguese (just as Haiti and the Dominican Republic became the separate possessions of France and Spain) even though they shared the same island mass. When the Dutch East Indies were granted their independence, becoming the vast and scattered republic of Indonesia in 1949, the Timorese people moved from owing allegiance to two distinct colonial powers (Portugal and Holland) to a situation where it was two political systems (continuing colonialism in the East and post-colonialism in the West) that determined their everyday lives. And when Indonesia looked around to see where it needed to tidy up scattered borders, its eye fell naturally and at once on East Timor.

It was only after the 'carnation revolution', which swept away the last of Portugal's dictators in 1974, that an opportunity presented itself. The new administration in Lisbon no longer had the appetite for ruling distant possessions especially when, as in East Timor, various factions began jostling and fighting them (and each other) for power. Portugal withdrew and, almost immediately, Indonesia pounced. In December 1975, everything was ready. Just by chance, President Gerald Ford and Secretary of State Henry Kissinger were in Jakarta on a regional visit, their visit giving a seal of approval to the Indonesian regime, which was seen by the USA as a player of great strategic importance in the vacuum left by the Vietnam debacle; here was a bulwark against communism, a nation to befriend. On the very eve of the invasion of East Timor Kissinger, fully aware of what was about to happen, went on the record with a statement telling the world how he 'understood' Indonesia's position on Timor. And binding commitments were made to re-supply Indonesia with all the military hardware it might need after it had completed its operation.

Australia was another key player in this squalid episode. East Timor had given immense support to Australia during the Second World War. For all that, Prime Minister Gough Whitlam stated in 1974 that he believed 'an independent East Timor would be an unviable state and a potential threat to the region'. Although he went on to declare his opposition to the use of force, Indonesia drew great strength from his statement. When the invasion took place a mere three months later, Australian Foreign Minister Gareth Evans shrugged off all criticism of it. 'The world is a pretty unfair place,' he said dismissively. Several years later, when President Clinton was attempting to take a more moderate and critical position with the Jakarta regime, Paul Keating, the then Prime Minister of Australia, was fierce in his denunciation of this new US stance. He spoke warmly of the 'stability' offered by Indonesia's President Suharto and described it as 'the single most beneficial strategic development to have affected Australia and its region in the past 30 years'. He even argued that it would be better to maintain a silence on the question of the Indonesian government's record on human rights.

The Roman Catholic Church too treated the annexation without demur. There were between four and five million Catholics in Indonesia. In the eyes of Rome they gave the Church a strategic position at the very gateway to South East Asia, a continent the Church had always found so challenging. What's more, though amounting to a mere 2 per cent of the population, Roman Catholics held a number of powerful positions in the Indonesian administration at that time. In the period immediately following the Portuguese withdrawal, there was civil chaos in East Timor as various factions jostled for power. It was obvious that this strife was being whipped up by Indonesian intelligence operatives. One of the factions contending for power was considered by the Roman Catholic bishop of Dili, Dom José Joaquim Ribeiro, to be a communist group and, for that reason alone, he refused to attempt to mediate a settlement. That was in 1975. His refusal was a lost opportunity of monumental proportions. It was probably the last, if not the only, chance of saving East Timor from what was about to happen.

And so, with the broad agreement of all the major powers that had their own vested interests in the new republic, Indonesia annexed East Timor as its twenty-seventh province. It should be pointed out that this did not please the rest of the world at all. The United Nations Security Council passed resolutions in 1975 and 1976 roundly

condemning their action. The General Assembly passed similar resolutions on a regular basis in the following years but nobody seemed to
have the will or the energy to turn those resolutions into action. From
1976, East Timor was closed to most outside observers and the local
resistance movement took to the mountains. By then, however, huge
damage and great suffering had been inflicted on the population of
East Timor.

Behind a blanket of silence, with all the world powers fully aware
of what was likely to be going on, the slaughter began. Out of a population of 700,000, 250,000 died between 1975 and 1979 (the same
number who died in Bosnia between 1991 and 1995, but in that case
out of a total population of 4 million). Whole villages were wiped out.
One observer later described the scene. 'All we could see were the
soldiers killing, killing, killing,' he said. Women and children were
not spared. This was surely a crime against humanity.

Secretary of State Henry Kissinger rebutted the arguments of those
who criticized the fact that the United States had provided 90 per cent
of the Indonesian army's fire power (and continued to do so after the
invasion) with the world-weary cynicism for which he became so well
known: 'Can't we construe [preventing] a Communist government in
the middle of Indonesia as self defence?' he asked plaintively. Daniel
Patrick Moynihan, the American ambassador to the United Nations,
was even more revealing when he came to write his memoirs. 'The
United States', he wrote,

wished things to turn out as they did, and worked to bring this
about. The Department of State desired that the United Nations
prove utterly ineffective in whatever measures it undertook. This
task was given to me, and I carried it forward with no inconsider-
able success.

These officials were supported in their views by the decision of the
Vatican to withdraw the head of the church in East Timor, Monsignor
Martinho da Costa Lopes (one of the first Timorese priests and Bishop
Bela's predecesor) for speaking out against the Indonesian atrocities.

The press colluded with these events. They maintained almost total silence on the plight of East Timor and seemed prepared to accept the version spun for them by their political masters of the time. The country was slowly and systematically being taken over by the Indonesians who were settling their own people on the best land and into the best jobs available. Local culture was being wiped out. And so it continued, after the initial massacres, for well over a decade. Then, suddenly, the whole world was shaken out of its stupor by a series of events that brought the plight of this tiny country back onto the news agenda.

The first of these was the visit of Pope John Paul II in October 1989. Until that moment, the Pope had been briefed on East Timor by his diplomatic corps and they had tended to put forward a very pro-Indonesian point of view. His visit, the only one undertaken during these difficult years by any world leader, opened his eyes both to the suffering of the people there and also to their determination to continue their struggle for independence from Indonesia. He was able to give solidarity to the remarkable young Bishop Belo of Dili, and also to many of the priests serving in his diocese. With his own eyes, he saw the tactics used by Indonesian troops to break up a demonstration. In his public utterances, using very coded language, it was clear he was refusing to give the Jakarta government any solace at all. His visit and his readiness, even in a covert manner, to show sympathy for the local cause proved to be a turning point for East Timor.

But it was a massacre which took place two years later that propelled East Timor to the front line of public awareness. Two hundred and fifty children were mown down in the graveyard of the Santa Cruz church in Dili. It was a cynical and cold-blooded act and done in the full light of day. Unfortunately for the Indonesian authorities, a television reporter had caught the whole event on film and was somehow able to smuggle his tapes out of East Timor. Those were the days when British television stations could still commission programmes based on serious investigative journalism. Max Stahl was in Dili making a programme for Yorkshire television which would eventually be called *Cold Blood: The Massacre of East Timor*. The footage of the Santa Cruz slaughter became central to this and was soon being shown all over Europe and the United States of America. It served as a wake-up call to the world.

An interest in the plight of the people of East Timor began to develop, fanned up by a press coverage that now became more intense and determined. The *Washington Post* was highly critical of the continued repression and mass arrests that took place in the months following the Santa Cruz massacre. And when Xanana Gusmão, the leader of the Timorese resistance, was caught and imprisoned in November 1992, it ran a series of editorials that criticized the 'arrogant and clumsy show of power' being displayed by Jakarta. It concluded that 'a wise Indonesian government should deal with Mr Gusmão in a political process', before asking: 'How can it be in Indonesia's interests to remain a colonial power?' Even the *Reader's Digest* got in on the act in February 1996 with a sympathetically drawn profile of Bishop Belo. This reached 100 million readers throughout the world, despite an Indonesian ban on the article.

In October 1996 came the unexpected announcement that Bishop Belo and José Ramos-Horta, chief international spokesman of East Timor's resistance movement, had been nominated to receive the Nobel Prize for Peace. The citation minced no words. It spoke directly of Indonesia's systematic oppression of the people of East Timor, the massive loss of life due to starvation, epidemics, war and terror. It recognized the way Belo and Ramos-Horta had sought a way forward through non-violence and dialogue with the Indonesian authorities. And it honoured the sustained and self-sacrificing contributions of the nominees on behalf of a small but oppressed people.

This award caught Washington off guard. President Clinton, in the middle of his bid for re-election, had the support of a number of business leaders with considerable financial interests in Indonesia. Consequently, the Nobel announcement caused some embarrassment though nobody, certainly not his opponent Senator Dole, could claim any moral high ground in the matter. There were strong and deep-seated civil as well as military ties with the Indonesian economy.

Just as revealing were the continuing negative responses from the

Vatican. Top officials there had shown constant impatience with the claims of East Timor. In 1981, six years after the Indonesian invasion, Dom Martinho of Dili had had a sharp exchange with Secretary of State Cardinal Casaroli, and had blurted out his objection. 'In matters of theology I believe the Vatican is infallible and I am obedient,' he said before continuing, 'but in matters of politics you are only human and you are wrong about East Timor.' Soon afterwards, he was removed from office and went into exile. When the 35-year-old Belo was appointed to replace him, there were strongly voiced objections from those officials in the Curia who favoured maintaining close ties with Indonesia. When, in 1984, Belo called for a cease-fire and greater autonomy for East Timor 'as a first step', the Papal Nuncio stepped in with a sharp rebuke and advised him to stick to his pastoral work. Even when the Pope had, during his visit, given every appearance of sympathy for Belo's leadership and the cause of the East Timor people, a small group of diplomats in the Vatican kept the question of East Timor at bay. When Belo was summoned to the Secretariat of State in late 1990, he was kept waiting 15 days by officials who gave no reason for the delay. When eventually given an appointment, he was kept waiting in an ante-room for two hours before being told to go away and come back the following day. Belo left in disgust and never came back at all. And he was still attracting opposition in Rome as late as 1996, but by then (having receiving the Nobel Prize) it had become politically impossible to remove him. Despite kind words from various cardinals and the Pope himself, Belo's (and East Timor's) problems with the Holy See rumbled on and on.

By the mid-1990s, there was a perceptible shift in public opinion with expressions of support coming from a number of directions. In 1995, the World Court confirmed that the people of East Timor were entitled to their internationally recognized right to self-determination. The United States, however, which didn't in any case accept the authority of this body, was far more concerned lest free elections in East Timor might call into question Indonesian ownership of the Timor Gap. Ownership of this potentially rich offshore area was shared between Australia and Indonesia under an agreement signed in December 1989. By the mid-1990s, various oil companies were announcing a multi-billion-dollar natural gas project centred in the Timor Gap. It followed that no one from the business sector wanted their investments threatened in any way.

Even the United Nations, which had passed one resolution after another in support of East Timor, dragged its heels in the mounting pressure for a solution of the problem. In February 1989, Bishop Belo wrote a passionate letter to Secretary General Javier Perez de Cuellar in which he pleaded for a UN-backed referendum to allow the people of East Timor to shape their own destiny. It took five years to get an answer to that letter. The new Secretary General, Boutros Boutros Ghali, wrote: 'The United Nations is committed to make every effort for a final, just, comprehensive and internationally acceptable solution.'

The period between the visit of the Pope and Belo's Nobel Peace Prize (1989–1996) was the time when it became more and more evident that East Timor was destined to enjoy a free future. Events moved with ever greater speed after the downfall of President Suharto of Indonesia in 1998. His successor, President Habibie, agreed to take part in a UN-brokered round of negotiations between Portugal and Indonesia. To everyone's surprise, in January 1997, his government raised the possibility of independence for East Timor for the first time. Soon afterwards, the resistance leader Xanana Gusmão was released from prison where he had languished since 1992. The United Nations agreed to send a peacekeeping force to oversee the transition period to self-rule. This produced a savage reaction from the Indonesian forces as they withdrew from their bases in East Timor, with an estimated 3–5,000 people killed in acts of sadistic savagery committed with apparent impunity.

When a UN International Commission of Inquiry issued a report in 2000 calling for a human rights tribunal under UN auspices 'to try and sentence those accused of serious violations of fundamental human rights and international humanitarian law', a call echoed by Amnesty International and the UN Mission stationed in East Timor, there was little appetite for the proposed measure. The UN Secretary General, Kofi Annan, despite receiving from his own observer mission 'a virtual library of evidence establishing the conspiracy between the Indonesian military and locally operating militias', refused to endorse their recommendation and the matter was allowed to drop.

One last word concerns the involvement of the United Kingdom government. As late as 23 September 1999, two weeks after the European Union had imposed an embargo on arms sales, three days after the UN peacekeeping force had landed in East Timor, and well after it had been revealed that these aircraft had been deployed again and again over East Timor, the Labour government continued to deliver Hawk jets to Indonesia. Indeed, under New Labour, Britain became the leading supplier of arms to Indonesia, despite the strong protests of Amnesty International, Indonesian dissidents, and Timorese victims. It was Robin Cook, whose clarion call for a new 'ethical foreign policy' had been so widely welcomed when he took up his new responsibilities, who explained that 'the government is committed to the maintenance of a strong defence industry, which is a strategic part of our industrial base'.

Perhaps the best summing up of this whole sorry story comes in the words of a senior diplomat who described the 'dilemma' facing the great powers succinctly when he said: 'Indonesia matters and East Timor doesn't.' For all that, after a quarter of a century of blood, strife and international neglect, East Timor became independent on 1 January 2000.

3 Eritrea

Eritrea is Africa's newest country. A referendum was held in April 1993 and, by a massive majority of the popular vote, a new nation was created and our atlases were once more out of date. At the same time, a war of attrition that had lasted over 30 years, came to an end.

Eritrea is about the size of England and sits alongside the Red Sea. Its neighbours are Sudan, Ethiopia and Somalia, which all cluster around it on the land mass of Africa. Just across the narrow sea lie the lands of Yemen and the Gulf States. For many decades its strategic importance sprang from the fact that it lay so near the trade routes opened up by the Suez Canal. Later on, it turned out that the clear air of its upper altitudes proved almost perfect for the listening devices so beloved of our intelligence-gathering bodies in those pre-satellite, pre-computer-chip days. It, together with other states in the Horn of Africa, became hotly contested territory in the days of the Cold War with Washington and Moscow vying furiously for influence and predominance there. Ethnically, it lies across the 'fault line' between Arab and African peoples; its population is shared evenly between the religions of Islam and Christianity.

All of this made Eritrea a political football. It has suffered ill treatment at the hands of virtually all who have set their designs on it. Its own legitimate interests have been overridden, sometimes wantonly, again and again. International law has proved impotent, the United Nations has colluded with those perpetrating its ills, the international community has been complicit in the injustices from which it has suffered. It offers a sorry catalogue of woes and makes a very strong case for a radical reform of the way we address situations of conflict. All our appeals to 'the rule of law' and 'the sovereignty of the state' have proved totally inadequate in the case of Eritrea.

By the end of the nineteenth century, Eritrea had become an Italian colony. The 1884–5 Berlin Conference had divided Africa up among the great powers of the day and it was the British who invited Italy to seize the port city of Massawa. Thus began a series of military actions that led to the signing of a treaty by Ethiopia and Italy in 1889. Whatever one thinks of the 'scramble for Africa', there can be no doubts that Italy's claims to Eritrea were as clear-cut as any being made by France, Germany, Belgium, Britain or Spain for their respective territories. In any case, by 1897, there was an Italian civil governor of Eritrea and the capital was moved to Asmara in the more congenial highlands. This new acquisition became the launching pad over the following half century for attempts to establish an Italian empire in Africa to include Somaliland, Libya and (disastrously) Abyssinia.

The Italian pretensions to an African empire were shattered by the events of the Second World War. A pitched battle at Keren, one of Eritrea's major cities, saw the defeat of the Italians, an event that

marked the end of their imperial aspirations. It left the British with
the administration of Italy's former possessions. They began immediately to 'asset-strip' the whole region to help pay their war bills. This
denuded Eritrea of its entire infrastructure, particularly its railway
and its port installations. And it made the country uninteresting to
anyone who might seek to take it over. So it could have surprised no
one when, in 1948, the Four Powers Commission set up to find a way
forward for Eritrea failed to come up with a firm recommendation.
Responsibility was passed over to the United Nations.

The Emperor Haile Selassie, who'd been in exile in England during the Italian possession of Abyssinia (Ethiopia), was returned to his
capital in 1941 and immediately set his eyes upon Eritrea. Ethiopia had
no direct access to the sea and, since the Emperor had grand designs
on making his nation the strongest and most successful in Africa, it
was inevitable that Eritrea came to figure greatly in his plans.

In 1949 a UN Committee of Enquiry was sent to sort out the future
of Eritrea and, after seemingly endless wrangles, decided three
years later that it should be federated with Ethiopia. This suited
Haile Selassie very well and he set about using this new relationship to serve his longer-term goals. When the highlands of Eritrea
were discovered to offer almost perfect conditions for intelligence-
gathering, the United States of America set about making the most
of this. It negotiated a 25-year contract with the Ethiopian government and established a base at Kagnew that allowed it to tap radio
signals from Moscow, the Arab world and Israel. This arrangement
also brought the Horn of Africa firmly within the American sphere of
interest. When the Russians began to take an interest in neighbouring Somalia, the Americans sought to match and outbid their rivals'
attempts to dominate the region. Their base at Kagnew, together with
the levels of interest being shown by the Russians, soon turned the
Horn of Africa into a key arena for the struggle between East and West
in the old Cold War days.

Haile Selassie knew exactly how to turn this situation to his advantage. By 1962, he had engineered the dissolution of the Eritrean
parliament. He had already seen to it that Amharic, the language

of Ethiopia, became the favoured language of instruction and public service. He had also placed his own trusted officials in Asmara
and other key cities. So the stage had been well prepared for the formal annexation of Eritrea by its Ethiopian neighbour. No one raised
a voice in protest. Not the United Nations; nor the Organization of
African Unity which, with a considerable injection of funds by the
Ethiopian government, had been enticed to set up its headquarters in
1963 in Addis Ababa; nor any of the major powers. Nobody.

So Eritrea was hung out to dry. Naturally, a resistance formed
and the Eritrean People's Liberation Front (EPLF) was established
by those who would settle for nothing less than full autonomy. They
were ashamed of the decision their parliament had been forced to take
which led to the annexation of Eritrea by Ethiopia. And they were
angry that the outside world simply looked on while this act of piracy
occurred. They fought ferociously and made telling gains, forcing
their way to the very edges of Keren, Asmara and Massawa. By the
early 1970s they seemed to have Haile Selassie's mighty army on the
run. Then came disaster.

In 1974, Haile Selassie was swept out of power by the Derg, a military group headed by an intelligent and reasonable officer, General
Aman Andom. Soon, however, he and his closest collaborators were
themselves eliminated in a merciless purge that saw Mengistu Haile
Mariam emerge as the Derg's undisputed leader. If the *ancien régime*
of Haile Selassie had been beset with delusions of grandeur, his successor soon went even further. First of all, he increased his demands
on his American paymasters who were still clinging to the strategic
importance of the Kagnew tracking station at a time when, in all truth,
the evolution of satellite technology was fast making it redundant. But,
with the Soviet Union implanted in neighbouring Somalia, Washington felt it couldn't afford to abandon the Horn of Africa. It was this
that led them to hang on to Kagnew and, as a direct consequence,
they found themselves faced with endless demands for more and more
military hardware.

When the EPLF reached the outskirts of Asmara in early 1975,
Mengistu decided to use the full range of his military power in a

savage onslaught that led to thousands of deaths in and around the capital city and the burning of 110 villages, where further huge numbers of peasants were bayoneted or shot under suspicion of collaborating with the rebels. The Eritrean people had long put up with the presence of the Americans in their midst but now, on the wrong end of American-made rocket-propelled grenades, bombed by F-5 jets flown by pilots trained in the US, tracked down by US Mack trucks carrying soldiers armed with US-made mortars, machine guns and rifles, a huge revulsion set in. Washington itself began to feel uneasy at the mass executions and atrocities that were taking place. And yet the Jimmy Carter administration continued, and intensified, the policies of its predecessor.

Despite all this, by 1977 the EPLF controlled 95 per cent of Eritrea. This led Mengistu to make his most audacious move. In order to win more arms from the United States, he threatened to turn to Moscow. In May 1977 he did just that and the Russians welcomed him with open arms. Even though they were already supporting Siad Barre's regime in neighbouring Somalia, they jumped at the opportunity to replace their American Cold War foes in the far more interesting Ethiopia. The Somali President wasn't best pleased by this but did himself no favours by invading the Ogaden province of Ethiopia and expelling 1,700 Soviet advisers. This merely gave the Soviets a pretext to pull out of their commitments to Somalia and put all their efforts into bolstering their new Ethiopian friends. The scale of this support was mind-boggling.

In a six-week period, arms worth $1–2 billion were shipped to Addis Ababa and 12,000 Cuban combat troops along with 1,500 military advisers were deployed there. The force of these weapons was turned on the EPLF. Just a year or two after being bombed by American F-5s, the Eritreans were fired on by MIG-15s. After a relentless and ruthless campaign of saturation bombing, and in the face of a highly trained Russian-led armed force attacking by land, air and sea, the EPLF retreated into the mountains to lick its wounds and to regroup. It would be well over a decade, aided by the collapse of the Soviet Union, before its fighters were to regain the ground they'd lost.

They had many more traumatic moments to live through. Between 1978 and 1991, the Soviet Union had funnelled almost $9 billion to Ethiopia in arms, a total that was the equivalent of $5,400 for every Ethiopian man, woman and child. Very little of this was addressed to the famine which, at this very same time, afflicted the country and which was brought to the attention of the British public by the newsreader Michael Buerk. What irony that, in the very year the Addis regime chose to splash out $55 million on a celebration of the tenth anniversary of the revolution which brought it to power, Bob Geldof's Live Aid efforts (together with the responses of western governments) were responding to the humanitarian needs of the ordinary people of Ethiopia.

Mengistu's army had been 45,000 strong when he came to power. Under his rule, it grew to a staggering 250,000 (with a further 200,000 reserves). But the end was nigh. Mikhail Gorbachev came to power in 1985 with a determination to disentangle the Soviet Union from some of its costly commitments. He couldn't do this at once, however, and arms continued to flood in to Ethiopia at a rate that far outstripped its capacity to absorb them. It was only in 1989 that everything was set for a Soviet withdrawal.

The EPLF saw its chance and began with increasing self-confidence to emerge from their mountain fastnesses. They were incredibly focused. There was widespread admiration in the international community for the way they'd maintained a humanitarian programme throughout their worst times, programmes of education, health and welfare. These activities often had to be conducted underground or at night to avoid the notice of surveillance planes constantly probing their mountain retreats. The self-discipline was astonishing. This was truly a government-in-waiting yet they got no support from the outside world. The United States and the Soviet Union had, through their support for successive governments in Addis Ababa, brought the full force of their armaments industry against them. No one in the non-aligned world raised their case. The Organization of African Unity was wedded to Ethiopian interests and 'the sovereignty of borders', even though those borders had been established by a wanton decision on the part of the international community to hand Eritrea over to Ethiopia. The United Nations, which had created the problem in the first place, proved unwilling to address the matter despite repeated attempts by Eritrean diplomats to argue their case. Even non-governmental organizations were, for the most part, unwilling to help. One, when asked to provide food for people in desperate circumstances, retorted: 'You are asking us to feed the enemies of our friend. We don't do that.'

There was one exception in this sorry tale of disregard. A number of Protestant church agencies, alarmed at the mounting number of victims both of drought and war, came together in the late 1970s to form the Emergency Relief Desk (ERD). Its work grew till it became the largest humanitarian operation ever undertaken by church agencies. A disparate group of agencies somehow managed to mount and maintain what was effectively a 'war consortium' for well over a decade. Their senior officers often overstepped their authority and they undoubtedly acted beyond the norms of convention or the law. Relief and support for the humanitarian work of the EPLF were provided across the Sudanese border. It was implemented by thousands of anonymous Eritreans who staffed distribution centres, worked on the roads over which relief needed to be conveyed, and repaired trucks, 'often with no tools except their brains and bare hands'. Others kept the community records in the village committees and selected the beneficiaries. A number were killed in acts of selfless heroism. Drivers sacrificed their lives driving during daylight when Soviet planes were out hunting them down. This was a rare light and it shone in times of exceeding darkness.

There are two acts of savagery that we must recount. First, the story of the Falashas. As early as 1975, Israel's parliament decreed that the claim of this unusual group of people living in Ethiopia to be of Jewish descent be granted. A small trickle of them began emigrating to Israel. During the 1984-5 famine this became a flood, with some 15,000 allowed to relocate. But a far larger number still remained. When the Soviet Union's commitment began to wane in the late 1980s, Mengistu saw his opportunity to use the Falashas as a bargaining ploy. It would be a case of Israeli arms in exchange for Ethiopian Jews. This put the Americans in a quandary. They didn't want to disappoint the request from their Middle Eastern ally to secure this exchange. They turned a blind eye, supposing that the operation would amount to little more than the sending of light arms and uniforms to Addis. They were insistent that no heavy weapons should figure in this transaction. But their imprecations were to no avail.

When the EPLF resumed its forward progress and finally captured Massawa in 1990, the Ethiopians made one last strike against their old foe. They subjected the port to a relentless round of air strikes that left the city reeling and in ruins once again. Those who survived this blitzkrieg reported the use of a new kind of bomb that shredded the streets of Massawa. Cluster bombs, supplied to the Israelis by their American friends, had been used indiscriminately against the Eritrean people. This was a final ignominy and a dire warning about the way the arms trade can yield unintended, unwanted, unwarranted, but very real results.

The village of Badme revealed other worrying factors. Five years after achieving nationhood, a border dispute between Eritrea and Ethiopia in this most unprepossessing of places led to a fierce war which ended with 70,000 dead. It needed the presence of UN peacekeepers to introduce calm to the area. Eventually, a Boundary Commission considered the dispute and ruled in Eritrea's favour. But the incident proved just how purist and inflexible the leaders of the new Eritrea were. They had been schooled in the wilderness and had had one sole objective. Now they needed to learn the art of nation building, but seemed to find this difficult. There is clearly much left to do.

4 Haiti

In July 1991, leaders of the countries of Latin America met in Santiago, the capital of Chile. The whole continent had just emerged from a long period of military rule and this summit had as one of its main items of business the question of how the democratic and accountable forms of government they had begun to enjoy could be made sustainable. This was a heady moment in world politics. The Berlin Wall had come down and communist regimes were collapsing across Europe. It was already clear that there was now only one super-power and that it would demand democratic governance wherever it exerted its influence. Latin American leaders wanted to make the right noises from the very outset of this new world order.

There was an up-beat feeling at the Santiago summit and a fulsome promise was made that if one of their number should suffer a coup d'état at the hands of their military then the others would all rally in support. Among those present was President Jean-Bertrand Aristide of Haiti who, a mere three months after this meeting, was ousted ignominiously from office. A military junta went on to rule Haiti for the next three years. Throughout this period, there was a manifest failure on the part of the international community in general, and the Organization of American States in particular, to deal with this problem. Despite a great deal of fine talk, the Haitian crisis defied all attempts at solution and much of the subsequent trouble suffered by the Haitian people has been the direct result of the failure of imagination and political will shown at this time.

Aristide had received 67 per cent of the popular vote in an election held in December 1990. This gave him a very substantial mandate to govern but no one underestimated the determination of his opponents to prevent him making progress. The Duvalier dynasty had ruled Haiti from 1957 to 1986. There followed five years of chaotic government largely under military rule. Only when Aristide threw his hat in the ring did a way out of this disorder become possible. Aristide was a Roman Catholic priest and from a humble background. He could speak several modern languages and had a working knowledge of ancient tongues too. He was committed to the methods of Liberation Theology, raising people's awareness and emboldening them to participate themselves in solving the age-old problems they'd suffered from. Haiti's tiny elite owned most of the country's wealth and the peasant masses had been kept in poverty virtually since the country's independence in 1804. Aristide and his comrades sought to bring these rural populations into the equation. They saw the fall of Duvalier as a golden opportunity to make this happen.

At first, the Roman Catholic Church led the way. A series of initiatives and proclamations by its bishops appealed to all sectors of Haiti's population to focus on the important tasks facing them. But Duvalier's backers had not given up the struggle. The army kept a hold on government, turning a blind eye to the activities of various right-wing neo-fascist groups which were mutations of Duvalier's secret police, the Tontons Macoutes. When Aristide became the focus for the anger of reactionary Duvalierist forces, his bishops and also the Papal Nuncio got cold feet. Their drive for more participatory governance became muted and, as if in compensation for this, Aristide took up the challenge on his own, acquiring in the process the characteristics of a popular hero. There were several attempts on his life but, armed with the obvious support of rural and urban slum populations, he emerged triumphant. The warning signs were, however, only too evident.

The Roman Catholic hierarchy was faced with a problem. A priest who would normally be subject to their authority had become a head of state whose authority they would now have to honour. They dithered before giving public support to the election results. They became implacable enemies of the priest-President. This was a vital factor to set alongside the opposition Aristide faced from other quarters. The Haitian army, disenchanted Duvalierists, the American and Dominican governments all had motives for wanting to get rid of the new President. It was a mere matter of time before his inevitable downfall.

And yet things began well enough. In the seven opening months of Aristide's presidency there were real signs of progress. He also sought to bring Haiti's peasant population into the political equation by giving official status to the Créole language and the Voodoo religion. He promised a major overhaul of the health system, an investigation into political crimes, the decentralization of power away from Port-au-Prince, a continuing fight against corruption and a strengthening of ties with other (especially Caribbean) countries. Inflation was reined back and there was a steady trickle of inward investment. Aristide promised to respect private property and impose probity in the public finances. But his main commitment was to the agricultural sector with pledges to fight illiteracy, malnutrition and deforestation.

Under pressure from the International Monetary Fund, the Aristide government pruned jobs in the public sector by 8,000 (out of 42,000). It also put the national cement factory and the flour mills onto a regular basis before selling them to the private sector, all part of an IMF Structural Adjustment Policy. In return for these and similar actions, the international community promised aid but stalled again and again before turning fine words into action. The Americans, for example, waited four months before even making a pledge of financial assistance. Of the $82 million promised for the year 1991-2, they delivered a mere $12 million and that was for the express purpose of repaying debts incurred by the then current government and its predecessors. So not a cent could be applied to the pressing problems facing the new President. Nor was this all. In July 1991, Haiti put forward an application for $250 million to finance a number of development programmes as part of a strategy to lose its status as the only LAC (Less Advanced Country) in the Americas. Astonishingly, a group of nations (including the USA) came up with pledges that exceeded the amount asked for by $100 million. This money would go towards a reduction of the national debt, reforms of public sector institutions, and almost a hundred social and economic projects. No money would be given, however, until detailed technical studies had been made. There would be no time for such studies. Aid never flowed to Haiti and this allowed Aristide's opponents to accuse him of negligence and procrastination.

The coup came in September 1991. This heralded as long and dark a period as any previously experienced in Haiti's turbulent history. The army and its fascist militia were so repressive and life became so difficult that thousands of poor Haitians were driven to set sail in unseaworthy craft in the hope of making the shore of Florida. It's one of the grim aspects of this tragedy that no one ever counted the number of refugees who perished at sea. Not only that: when the United Nations eventually imposed sanctions on Haiti they hit the poorest people hardest. And the US coastguard vessels patrolling Haitian waters to supervise the sanctions were able to track down even the smallest boat and return its passengers to the ravaged and savaged land they were fleeing. Strangely, large oil tankers making for the one and only off-loading point near Port-au-Prince managed again and again to slip through the same blockade with impunity. The question of how to use sanctions in a targeted and effective way (soon to become an important aspect in the Iraqi crisis) was posed very sharply by the Haitian experience.

The deposed President Aristide spent most of his long exile in the United States. There he was subjected to the most intense barrage of criticism from Senator Jesse Helms and his Senate Foreign Relations Committee. This went as far as to produce 'evidence' (later proved a fabrication) from a Canadian hospital to suggest that Aristide was 'clinically manic-depressive'. Helms went as far as to describe the deposed President as 'psychotic' and 'a killer'. General Brent Scowcroft, one-time national security adviser to President Bush Senior, went even further, alleging that Aristide was 'a certifiable psychotic'. Meanwhile Brian Latell, the CIA's chief Latin American analyst, put his own boot in, telling reporters that Aristide had 'psychological disorders and has used thirteen kinds of medicine, especially Lithium and Haldol'. Cardinal Nicolas Lopez Rodriguez, head of the Roman Catholic Church in the Dominican Republic and President of the Latin American Episcopal Conference, declared himself implacably opposed to any plan to restore Aristide who, in his view, was 'inexperienced in politics, insensitive and incompetent'. Views such as these, with little or no authenticity and offered by those with barely disguised vested interests to defend, were faithfully reported in all the main newspapers and on television networks. Everyone seemed content to focus on Aristide's personality rather than on the question of a constitutional future for Haiti. There can be no doubt that this exercise in character assassination filled any prospect of returning Aristide to his functions with the inevitability of failure. And all the while this was taking place, an increasingly brutal military regime was going about its repressive activities with impunity.

At first, the United Nations passed responsibility for solving the dispute to its regional player, the Organization of American States.

Envoys were appointed, there was much to-ing and fro-ing, delega-
tions were even threatened with physical harm by Haitian fascist
groups, and time was wasted. Nothing came of these efforts. It took a
resolution of the Security Council and the acceptance of responsibility by the UN itself to move things forward. This led to peace talks
on Governor's Island, New York, which brought all the parties together, the first example of 'proximity talks' that were soon to be used
at Dayton, Ohio, to address the Balkan crisis. A significant factor
throughout this period was the warm personal friendship that grew
up between Aristide and President Clinton, who was even prepared
to denounce the CIA report on the Haitian President's mental condition. This changed atmosphere injected political will to the search for
a solution. It was undoubtedly helped by the constant arrival of waves
of boat-people who, with the blockade now lifted, began reaching the
shores of Florida in significant numbers.

The Governor's Island accord was a flawed agreement. It greatly
restricted Aristide's freedom of action (no bad thing) and gave general
amnesty to those who'd implemented and maintained the coup. It set
up a new government for Haiti but kept Aristide out of the country
until stability had been restored. For all its shortcomings, it was the
best deal available and was certainly better than some of the alter-
natives on offer. One, put forward by a senior United Nations agent,
rivalled the Owen–Vance plan later to be put forward for solving the
troubles in Bosnia-Herzegovina. This plan would have kept warring
factions apart by setting up an intricate set of reserved areas for each
of them. But Bantustanization rarely solves underlying problems and
it certainly wouldn't have in this case.

Aristide was widely condemned by the international community
for his apparent refusal to compromise during the Governor's Island
negotiations. The *Washington Post* demanded that he 'begin working
energetically with his enemies as well as his friends'. And *The Times*
echoed this from a London perspective: 'Haiti's robbed president
must learn to compromise,' it declared. What remains incredible in
all this was the refusal of anyone to analyse the critical paths showing
flexibility and readiness for compromise followed respectively by

Aristide and the military leadership. The former had made concession after concession. His opponents had made none. Indeed, they'd
tightened their oppressive control over a faltering Haiti, enjoyed a
close working relationship with the CIA, managed to turn economic
sanctions to their own benefit, and found huge amounts of extra resources from drug-running. They succeeded in all this without a hint
of compromise, yet they had the satisfaction of seeing their arch-en-
emy pilloried for his 'intransigence' by an international community
that had got tired of Haiti and just wanted to wash its hands of the
whole affair. Similar absolutist expectations are just as much on display towards the democratically elected leadership of the peoples of
Iran and Palestine. No doubt compromise is going to be needed, but
it takes two to talk and one isn't always aware of much in the way of
concession on the other side of the conversation.

Aristide was a broken figure when he was brought back by the
Americans in October 1994. He'd resigned from the priesthood and
was now married with a child. This undoubtedly robbed him of some
of the mystique with which his previous status had clothed him. He
was flown back in a helicopter supported by a force of 20,000 American troops. A tiny fraction of that number would have done but this
vast force impressed one fact on everyone. Aristide was now a puppet
of the Americans, his 'second coming' entirely due to the nation he
had so often criticized in the past. The one-time liberation theolo-
gian, so feared by right-wing ideologues in Washington, had now been
robbed of all his powers. A few short months were all that remained of
his period in office; he'd been in exile for three years and two months
of the five years of his mandate. It's interesting that he used his last
brief moment in power to implement two major initiatives. He dis-
banded the Haitian army (following the example of Costa Rica) and
his government opened diplomatic relations with nearby Cuba. The
first of these was to create its own problems in future years and would,
indeed, produce the events that saw his overthrow during his second
term in 2004. The second opened the way for the most significant
bilateral programme of medical, social and logistical support enjoyed
by Haiti during the troubled years it was yet to endure.

One of the bleakest moments during the coup came when Antoine Izméry, a well-known supporter of Aristide who was attending a Mass in downtown Port-au-Prince, was forcibly taken out of the church and murdered in cold blood on the street. The perpetrator of this deed, a man named Michel François, was later imprisoned for this and other atrocities. When Aristide was returned for a second term in 2001, François and other felons like Louis-Jodel Chamblain and Emmanuel Constant escaped and spearheaded the uprising that eventually ousted him in February 2004. Incredibly enough, the forcible removal of a democratically elected head of government by a bunch of indicted criminals was widely hailed by the international community as giving Haiti a new opportunity to get its act together. The logic is difficult to follow.

Throughout the long saga of Haiti's post-Duvalier search for a more just and open society, all the attention was focused on the personality of Jean-Bertrand Aristide. Few observers noted how he had to operate in a context where well-armed opponents who wanted to kill him made constant vigilance necessary and might even explain his drift towards self-protective mechanisms that were themselves odious and totally unacceptable. Nor was there much recognition that this 'democratically elected' President was obliged to operate for much of his time in office without a functioning legislature, with no justice system and none of the institutions of civil society that engender free and open discussion. The flow of international aid was regulated in a way intended to force his government to comply with policy objectives determined elsewhere. The downfall of Aristide was engineered by the very international system established to protect vulnerable countries from the whims and power-lust of their armed forces. This has been an unwholesome and troubling tale whose aftermath is still being played out in an acrimonious and increasingly despairing environment.

5 Iraq

On 20 March 2003, Neil Kinnock took part in the regular Thursday 'Conversations' at Wesley's Chapel. The overall purpose of these interviews is to explore values in public life, how people identify them and then go on to apply them in their daily lives. But on that day one subject dominated everyone's attention and it was inevitable that it would be discussed. For that was the day the war against Iraq began. It would be interesting to hear Kinnock's view on such a pressing matter.

He was unhesitating. He supported the Prime Minister's decision 150 per cent, he said (with a typical flourish). It was a job that needed finishing and Saddam Hussein could not be tolerated one day longer. Kinnock had been the leader of the Labour Party at the time of the First Gulf War and he'd been party to many briefings relating to that conflict. He knew that George Bush Senior had left unfinished business. He wished that it hadn't been Bush's son marching in to complete the task but this war was something that simply had to be done.

Such an out-and-out stance took everyone by surprise. As did what followed. Kinnock went on to say that Glenys, his wife, disagreed totally with him. For the first time in 30 years the two of them had come to diametrically opposed positions on a subject of consequence. They'd had to agree to live with their disagreement, accepting the sincerity and truthfulness with which each had reached their conclusions. Their dilemma was the one faced by the country at large on this particular issue.

Iraq was a crisis that dominated the early 1990s, one that played out in two movements. It was left unresolved in 1991. And, because it was in the oil-rich Middle East, a day was bound to come when there would have to be a closure. Before the second movement could materialize, however, 9/11 had taken place. That gave its own twist to the war, which was made to seem like a mere retaliation driven by wounded pride. Certainly the discussion of the war took place as if very little of Iraq's pre-9/11 history counted for much. The al-Qaeda attacks on New York and Washington had given a new point of departure for the discussion of conflict.

And yet the earlier history matters a great deal, especially the events that followed from the life of the prophet Muhammad. It might be said to have begun in the dim and distant seventh century when Ali, the son-in-law and cousin of the prophet Muhammad, was assassinated in the very moment he became the successor of the prophet. What's more, his own sons Hussein and Abbas were also killed by those who objected to their claims to the succession. Father and sons were buried in Najaf and Kerbala respectively. With their martyrdom, Shi'a Islam came into existence and these Iraqi shrines assumed an importance little short of that accorded to Medina and Mecca. These sites became important for those living on the nearby Persian plateau too and, when the Ayatollah al-Khomeini needed a refuge from those opposing him in Iran, it was in Kerbala that he found a spiritual home until he left for Paris several years later. It is difficult to over-emphasize the religious importance of this region for Shi'a Muslims.

Many centuries later, during the Ottoman Empire, Iraq constituted three provinces which were administered separately from Mosul, Baghdad and Basra. Modern Iraq was only created by a British geographer in the early part of the twentieth century when the British sought to secure a strong presence in the Middle East. So difficult was it, however, to forge a national identity between groups whose loyalties were overwhelmingly tribal that the British resorted to air power to maintain their hold. The RAF used Iraqi air space to conduct their training manoeuvres and it was here that Arthur 'Bomber' Harris first displayed a readiness to bomb civilian populations, as part of the drive to control the Iraqi people. T. E. Lawrence (Lawrence of Arabia) went further and suggested the use of poison gas to maintain order. It would be, in his view, cheap and effective. It is difficult to over-emphasize the tribal loyalties of the peoples of this area or the difficulties to be faced in forging them into a single people.

The puppet kings of Iraq were finally overthrown in 1958. Throughout the following 20 years, a time of great chaos, Saddam Hussein became an increasingly central figure. The Ba'ath party, to whose philosophy he subscribed, sought to wed a pan-Arabian political stance with a 'woolly' socialist programme. Its methods were severe and sought to achieve control through a 'terrorism of the mind'. Its victims could find a refuge only in their families or their faith, which became 'temporary havens of hate-filled religious sectarianism'. Strangely enough, Ba'athism is thought by some to have drawn heavily on Hobbes' *Leviathan*, where it is stated that 'every particular man is Author of all the Sovereigne doth; and consequently he that complaineth of injury from his Sovereigne complaineth of all that whereof he himself is Author; and therefore ought not to accuse any man but himself'. By this route, the Ba'ath party sought to create a 'mass society' in which individuals are uprooted and alienated from their past. This 'individualism of the masses' would be accompanied by the crushing of any notion of civil society. The systematic way this view of the world was imposed on the people of Iraq is key to any understanding of what followed.

And then there was the war with Iran (1980–88) which left almost a million dead. Alongside this should be seen the oppression of the Kurds and the use of chemical weapons. Five thousand Kurds died in Halabja in a mere 30 minutes. There's little doubt that the fear of the continued use of these weapons of mass destruction subdued the Kurds and drove Iran to seek an end to the war. Saddam Hussein was able, of course, to claim a 'victory' on both fronts. The effect of the devastating loss of so many young Iraqis during these years contributed greatly to the creation of 'a republic of fear' in Iraq.

There can be no doubt that Iraq was committed to the development of weapons of mass destruction. There was a definite and proven programme for creating a nuclear bomb and related missiles. Billions of dollars were spent on this and some 8,000 scientists were working on it at one time. The possession and use of chemical and biological weapons was also patent. In the course of the 1990s, the nuclear potential was discovered by UN inspectors and slowed down before ultimately being stopped. But to this day no one can be sure about whether there are hidden stockpiles of chemical or biological weapons. Since a sack of flour dropped on Kurds from a helicopter induced widespread panic and flight on one occasion, it is obvious how effective the threat of such weapons would be and how easy it would be to hide them. In Andrew and Patrick Cockburn's book *Saddam Hussein*, there's a chapter called 'Saddam fights for his long arm'. It tells the story of the twistings and turnings of Saddam Hussein as he strove to hide first the existence and then the extent of his weapons industry from the UN inspectors during the 1990s. 'After sifting through thousands of pages and documents and the reports of hundreds of hours of interviews,' they write, 'it was still impossible [for UN inspectors] to account for as many as 150 bombs and warheads that had at one time been manufactured for the Iraqi air force.' This assessment, published in the days immediately prior to 11 September 2001, was offered by two long-time commentators on Iraq. Their observation should certainly be borne in mind by anyone trying to make sense of what happened afterwards. There can be no reasonable doubt about Iraq's commitment to the production of weapons of mass destruction in the years following the First Gulf War.

At the conclusion of that war, the Shi'ites and the Kurds rose up against Saddam Hussein, confident that they'd be given support and backup in their attempts to overthrow him. President Bush Senior had said in February 1991: 'I appeal to the Iraqi military and the Iraqi people to take matters into their own hands – to force Saddam Hussein the dictator to step aside . . . and to rejoin the family of nations.' The people took this as a promise they'd be helped if they made any such effort. They did. And they weren't. Irony of ironies, it seems that a high-level coup attempt was about to be made against Saddam Hussein by a group of his senior army officers. The popular uprisings that followed President Bush's broadcast appeal took them by surprise and diverted their attention. So the moment was lost.

The United States then took a fateful decision to maintain the sanctions that had been imposed on Iraq for the duration of its occupation of Kuwait. This was to have dreadful outcomes. Sanctions hit ordinary people the hardest and gave Saddam Hussein lots of free propaganda. It's been estimated that half a million Iraqi children died as a result of the deprivations caused by these measures. One official put it very succinctly; 'Sanctions are undermining the moral credibility of the United Nations,' he said. Yet there were few voices raised against them in the outside world. As the Cockburns put it:

Dry statistics detailing remorselessly escalating infant mortality rates or the percentage of underweight children, or even the death of a little boy – Hussein Ali Majhoul – for want of a working truck to drive across town, could not jump-start an international furore over the sanctions policy.

In the light of the huge anti-war demonstrations that took place on 15 February 2003, it seems fitting to ask why so little fuss had been made at the monstrous losses that resulted from these economic measures whose victims were always innocent civilians.

The Second Iraq War seemed inevitable from the moment the dust had settled after the 9/11 attacks. So many issues got confused as President George W. Bush unleashed his anti-terror rhetoric on an unsuspecting world. Axis of evil, smoke 'em out, settle old scores, bring 'em on – this folksy discourse clothed the determination on the American administration's part to deal with the problem of Iraq. This served the United Kingdom's need to be seen to be taking action and Prime Minister Blair, the 'man of action' par excellence, chose to get involved. Was he the President's poodle or was he trying to ride an enraged tiger? The role of the United Nations, the posturing of President Chirac, the sexed-up dossiers, the allegations and counter-allegations about deliberately misleading the public, gung-ho speeches, the increasing inevitability of armed intervention, the failure to find weapons of mass destruction, the introduction of the 'regime change' justification, the failure of 'just war' discourse to meet the case, the death of David Kelly, the Hutton enquiry, the resignations of Clare Short and Robin Cook, of Andy Gillingham and Greg Dyke, the widespread alienation of Muslims in the General Election – all of these (and many more) were factors surrounding this deeply divisive war. But, in all of it, it is surely to be regretted that there was generally very little awareness of so much that had preceded it. The events of 11 September allowed a situation to emerge where people took sides as if there had been no previous history. Yet no one should have been allowed to forget Saddam Hussein's repressive rule, his senseless war with Iran, the use of chemical weapons against the Kurds, the destruction of habitat and culture of the Marsh Arabs, the invasion of Kuwait, the development of weapons of mass destruction, the ethnic cleansing of tens of thousands of Shi'as in the aftermath of the First Gulf War, the expulsion of UN weapons inspectors, the failure of the United Nations, the huge cost in human life of its sanctions policy, the unlawful extension of that policy by the United States, or the corruption of very senior United Nations officials who enriched themselves out of the proceeds of the oil-for-food policy. Nor should anyone forget how the righteous indignation displayed in the huge demonstrations of 15 February 2003 were preceded by a long period of soul-less apathy towards the victims of the massive injustices in the 12-year period that preceded the war. But no one can doubt, for all that preceded it, that 9/11 represented a new base line for any consideration of Iraq.

It seems as if people's consciences are touched only when a crisis has broken. There is so little readiness to read the signs of the times and foresee the way these crises are going to emerge. The anti-war demonstrations were certainly impressive. But it was all so reactive. By the time people took to the streets it was far too late. How can public opinion be engaged in the issues that build up to such crises? How can we address conflict and the causes of conflict before they erupt into the end-game scenario? Everything was in place for this Iraq war during the 1990s. Admittedly, the 9/11 episode gave extra impetus to what happened as well as a discourse of ugly revenge that we could have done without. But the war, when all is said and done, was the culmination of a process which, all along the way, produced one offensive and distressful moment after another. It was self-indulgence to wait till the writing was on the wall before we put our spectacles on to read its messages.

No wonder Neil and Glenys Kinnock were able to reach such diametrically opposed conclusions. No issue has more deeply divided public opinion in recent times than this one. The four vignettes that follow show the same polarization of views.

The Master of a Cambridge College was sitting next to Hans Blix at dinner. Blix had headed the UN weapons inspectorate and had protested long and loud at not having been allowed to complete his job before hostilities broke out. Conversation inevitably touched on the Iraq war. The Master, an implacable opponent of the war, expected to find Blix in support of his stance. Something very different proved to be the case. Blix made it clear that he was only a technical expert and not a politician. If he had had political decisions to make, he added, he might well have come to the same conclusions as those who went to war. This declaration stupefied everyone within hearing.

On another occasion, when Robert McNamara (former US Secretary of Defense, former President of the World Bank and former President of the Ford Company) addressed a group of British parliamentarians, the chair was taken by Robin Cook, who had resigned from his post as Foreign Secretary over the war and had become one of its outspoken critics. With Cook sitting immediately alongside him, McNamara made it clear that he considered that Tony Blair, far from being a lapdog to George W. Bush, had had a very significant effect on him. The American people were profoundly unilateralist, he said, something he felt to be radically wrong. He expressed deep personal gratitude to the Prime Minister for his courage and leadership. Cook and McNamara, sitting alongside one another, offered another visible picture of the way intelligent and honourable people had reached opposite conclusions.

And then there was the matter of the role of the Attorney General, Lord Goldsmith. Was he leaned on to produce the judgment about the legal basis for conducting the war, he was asked? He refuted this suggestion with vigour and made it clear that it was advice offered on the same basis as all other legal counsel he'd given in a law career of 30 years. He had always believed, and still believed, that the war was legal. What's more, he'd since had occasion to speak to UN legal officers, and they too believed there was an adequate legal basis for going to war and they'd advised the Secretary General accordingly. This outright statement was made to a group that included some very vociferous opponents of the war. They heard it with respect though it didn't alter their views one iota.

Ian McEwan's *Saturday* appeared early in 2005 to much critical acclaim. The novel deals with a series of events that take place on Saturday, 15 February 2003, the day of the mass demonstration against the impending war in Iraq. The main character, Henry Perowne, is a neuro-surgeon and his personal agenda constantly engages with the issue that brought so many people in protest to the streets of London on that one day which, more than any other, highlighted the deep divisions within British society on the question of this war. Perowne's children, a guitar-strumming son and a high-brow literary daughter, display deep unhappiness about the war. Perowne himself, a very cool and detached character, seems more interested in assessing and analysing the available evidence than in coming to a view on the matter.

At one stage, he remembers one of his patients, an Iraqi intellectual who'd been imprisoned by Saddam Hussein's henchmen. This gentle, scholarly man was thrown into a stinking prison cell with 25 others, and held without any charge. He'd been tortured and brutalized and he'd been well aware of the insufferable treatment of men and women around him. Perowne's memory of the encounter ends with the conclusion that the Iraqi professor put on it. 'Everyone hates it,' he said.

You see, it's only terror that holds the nation together, the whole system runs on fear, and no one knows how to stop it. Now the Americans are coming, perhaps for bad reasons. But Saddam and the Ba'athists will go. And then, my doctor friend, I will buy you a meal in a good Iraqi restaurant in London.

Whatever opinion one holds about the outbreak of the war, there can be little doubt that far too little thinking had been done about the post-war reconstruction needs of Iraq. The wholesale dismantling of Ba'athism left almost nothing to build with. And that created a vacuum which terrorist and sectarian groups could exploit. And all this has led to a dreadful loss of life in one atrocity after another. Estimates vary about how many Iraqis have died in the aftermath of the war. Three years after the cessation of hostilities one report suggested a total of 35,000. Doubled, as other reports suggest, it would give an average of 25,000 victims per annum. This is a gruesome statistic to contemplate, an atrocious cost to this war. But no one should forget the even more gruesome statistics that cover the 12-year period between the two phases of the Gulf War. It is commonly agreed that half a million children died during those years because of the way sanctions hit Iraq. Add an undisclosed number of adults, and also the victims of Saddam Hussein's campaigns against Shi'a Muslims and all other opponents, and it's not difficult to imagine a figure twice as high. If such speculation is anywhere near the mark, then an average of 80,000 people died per annum in a period whose consequences can be directly attributed to the refusal of the international community to complete its task in 1991. And these massive losses of innocent civilians in Iraq happened with very little protest in those countries which were to take to the streets in such huge numbers in February 2003.

There is no tidy line to draw under the Iraq crisis. Post-war events continue to offer 'evidence' to buttress the case put forward by both supporters and opponents of the intervention. A government has been elected and a massive military presence shows resolution on the part of the international community to stand in solidarity with the people of Iraq. On the other hand, the mistreatment (torture) of prisoners by occupying troops, the long-term prisoners in Guantanamo Bay and the absence of any apparent co-ordinated post-war plan for the re-development of Iraq – all these point to an ongoing and increasingly desperate scene. Meanwhile, the number of civilian deaths mounts alarmingly. Iraq seems perilously close to civil war. Chaos reigns.

6 Rwanda

There it was, the highlight of the in-flight programme of entertainment, the recently released film *Hotel Rwanda*. It chronicles the remarkable exploits of Paul Rusesabagina who, from his Kigali hotel, somehow managed to protect the lives of dozens of people who would otherwise have been slaughtered. It really does seem odd that such a saga of human suffering should be turned into a film. Its story line was drawn from a book by journalist Philip Gourevitch with the extraordinary title *We Wish to Inform You That Tomorrow We Will Be Killed with Our Families*. This book, more than anything else, brought the international community face to face with the appalling indifference and catastrophic ignorance that allowed 800,000 people to die in acts of genocide within the space of 100 days in the spring and early summer of 1995.

Nobody flinches now at the use of the word genocide to describe those atrocities. Yet there was great reluctance to use it at the time because, once that genie pops out of its bottle, there are consequences that some people prefer to avoid. The 1948 Genocide Convention makes it obligatory for all signatories to intervene and take action once the 'g' word has been used. The United States of America, for its own reasons, wished to avoid this at all costs. They had only just endured the sight of American soldiers being killed and dragged around the streets of Mogadishu, capital of Somalia. The Clinton administration did not want further embroilment in faraway Africa so they skirted around the use of the word genocide with embarrassing awkwardness. They began by recognizing that 'acts of genocide may have occurred' but refused to say just how many such acts would amount to genocide proper. This *danse macabre* around the issue was taking place at the very height of the slaughter. It was weird to say the least. But then, both Rwanda and the United States were Johnny-come-latelies to such matters; they'd become signatories to the Convention only in 1975 and 1989 respectively.

Rwanda was originally inhabited by the Twa people, cave-dwelling pygmies who now represent a mere 1 per cent of the population. It is reckoned that hundreds of years ago (there is no recorded history) Hutus arrived in this beautiful land-locked territory from the south and from the west. The Tutsis came from the north. While there are features that distinguish them from each other, they have co-existed for so long and there has been so much inter-marriage and social change that no one could confidently identify their respective communities with much accuracy. It was 1894, a decade after the Berlin Conference that divided Africa among the European colonial powers, before a white man set foot in Rwanda. Soon the territory was being administered by the Germans although, after the First World War, this responsibility passed to Belgium. Both Germans and Belgians chose to rule Rwanda through the minority Tutsis. On the whole they'd been cattle owners, as opposed to the Hutus who were farmers, but this distinction had become increasingly blurred with the passing of the years. The Belgians, possibly because they themselves came from a society divided between a Flemish minority and a Walloon majority, issued identity cards that defined citizens according to their ethnicity. This was to play its own part in the gruesome events that were to occur well after the Belgians had left.

The period 1959–1962 was crucial to all that was to happen later. These years saw Rwanda's transition from colonial status to independence and its ruling group from the minority Tutsis to the majority Hutus. Central to these developments was the beating up of a Hutu official, a political activist, named Dominique Mbonyumutwa. Accounts varied as to whether he'd been killed or merely wounded but this incident proved the tinder that set passions aflame. Soon, bands of roving Hutus were seeking out Tutsis, torching their homes and killing their victims. This 'wind of destruction', as it came to be called, took place in the full view of Belgian troops who did nothing to prevent it. Indeed, they glorified the slaughter by referring to it as 'democratization'. And they went on to mount elections which, overseen by Hutus, ensured a massive Hutu victory. Tutsis were ejected from their homes, deprived of their jobs, arrested arbitrarily, and driven into exile. The Belgians had switched ethnic sides on the very eve of independence. This was declared in 1962 and Grégoire Kayibanda was inaugurated as the first President of the new republic.

There could be no doubt that this arrangement contained the seeds of its own grim demise. Indeed, a UN Commission at the time declared that the Rwandan revolution had brought about 'the racial dictatorship of one party', replacing 'one type of oppressive regime with another'.

Two things need to be noted from this masquerade. First, there is no such thing as an 'age-old' dispute between Tutsis and Hutus. The troubles between them were clearly the result of Belgian colonial policy, which chose to organize the country along ethnic lines and was prepared to shift its allegiance from one side to the other when it suited it. And, second, it was clearly understood at the time that a

dangerous situation had been created by the very nature of the revolution that brought Hutus to power. Rwanda was born to die. And
nobody can claim ignorance after the event.

Atrocities continued through the 1960s but a new dimension was
added in 1972–3 by events in neighbouring Burundi. There, a mirror
image of Rwanda, it was a military government run by Tutsis that was
keeping a Hutu minority in subjection. Violent purges against edu-
cated Hutus led to 100,000 deaths and twice as many refugees, many
of whom fled to Rwanda. This, in turn, allowed President Kayibanda
to turn the screws further on his own Tutsis. The death toll this time
was relatively low but there was a mass exodus of Tutsis from Rwanda.
The whole area became very destabilized and everyone welcomed the
overthrow of Kayibanda by Major General Juvénal Habyarimana in
1973. He called off the attacks on Tutsis and promoted a programme
of national 'development'. There was such universal relief that people
forgot that it was Habyarimana who had conducted the pogroms
against Tutsis so recently. The honeymoon period was destined not
to last very long.

Groups of young men began roving Tutsi areas bent on murder.
Soon the *interahamwe*, as they were called, had become a force to
be taken seriously and the unofficial arm of state terror. Their efforts
were whipped up by the official Radio Rwanda and, long before the
final surge of hatred against the Tutsis in 1994, they had soaked themselves in blood. Yet the international community, taken in by Habyarimana's ready espousal of the vocabulary of 'development' (then very
much in vogue), poured money into his coffers. It was bizarre, this
mixture of slaughter within and oodles of money from without.

But the international community did apply enough pressure to
force the President to sign a peace accord with the rebel Rwanda
Patriotic Front (RPF). Under its terms, the Tutsis who had fled the
country were to be allowed safe passage home. Elections were promised and the United Nations invited to oversee the implementation of
the agreements.

This agreement, the Arusha Accord, was to prove a trigger for the
end-game. First of all, it led to the death of President Habyarimana in

a plane crash, an event brought about by Hutus who could not bear to accommodate the Tutsis they'd become so bent on destroying. His death was followed very quickly by the assassination of ten Belgian soldiers who were fronting the UN force sent in accordance with the agreement. This led to the early withdrawal of the Belgians and disarray among the remaining troops. So, with the President out of the way and the UN troops reeling, the slaughter began. No one could pretend they didn't see it coming. Indeed, the UN commander, General Dallaire, had sent a very explicit message to New York in which he reported in circumstantial detail a plan to exterminate Tutsis. Yet nothing was done. And as the killings grew in number and the evidence of genocide became irrefutable, General Dallaire became more and more frustrated. He urged the UN to give him just 5,000 troops – enough, he said, to keep the factions apart. Instead, under pressure from Madeleine Albright, President Clinton's ambassador to the UN (and later Secretary of State), the number of troops was actually reduced to a miserly 270! In the end, when it was far too late, a number of African countries organized a military presence in Rwanda. Meanwhile, hundreds of thousands of Tutsis died. As Philip Gourevitch put it: 'their slaughter took place at nearly three times the rate of Jewish dead during the Holocaust. It was the most efficient mass killing since the atomic bombings of Hiroshima and Nagasaki.'

One astonishing feature of this massacre was the complicity of Church leaders, both Protestant and Catholic. It seems likely that Tutsis who took refuge in church premises were betrayed, flushed out, named and exposed to bloodthirsty *interahamwe* groups on the rampage. It may actually have been worse than that, with deliberate efforts being made to undermine the UN force's efforts to evacuate refugees, and even the coercing of girls for sexual purposes. All this while people were being butchered, cut apart with machetes, left maimed or dead, their bodies piled up in the streets or stuffed down wells or in canyons. It was a savagery that beggared belief.

The commitment to exterminate the Tutsis left the Hutu leadership short of a disciplined force to counter the RPF army that was advancing fast on Kigali. In the midst of great chaos, in mid-June 1994, the French government (with the backing, let it be noted, of a United Nations resolution) sent in a military force to relieve pressure on the Hutus. It was ostensibly a humanitarian mission and was greeted wildly by *interahamwe* fighters and the Hutu population at large. In effect, the 'humanitarian' aspect of the French arrival was merely a cover for the shipment of huge quantities of arms brought over the Zaire border for the use of the Rwanda government in its genocidal drive against the Tutsis. The sight of these blue-bereted French soldiers conducting their 'rescue' mission when almost a million Tutsis were already dead, their corpses not yet decently buried, and with General Dallaire standing by watching them arrive with impunity after his own request for timely support had been so crushingly refused, must represent an almost unrivalled act of cynicism in modern times. When, a little later, France broke ranks with the rest of the world and restored aid to Zaire's dictator President Mobutu (who was a prime beneficiary of the Rwanda massacres) they were merely compounding that cynicism and showing off their almost uncritical support for the Hutu power-holders.

In the meantime, in the face of a resolute RPF advance, and fearing reprisals, Hutus began fleeing across the Zaire border in huge numbers. As Philip Gourevitch puts it:

> this was the largest and speediest mass flight across an international border in modern history, and although it included whole formations of *interahamwe*, military units, town councils, and the civilian throngs who had strewn the church at Nyarubuye and the rest of Kibungo with corpses, those who fled were indiscriminately received with open arms by UN and humanitarian agencies and accommodated as refugees in giant camps.

These camps soon caught the imagination and touched the hearts of the world. They were vast and the suffering of the people within them was palpable. Such concentrations of human misery had become familiar parts of our landscape in the late twentieth century. From Sudan to Mozambique they seemed to stretch out across the

length of a whole continent. But these camps at Goma, established in
the immediate aftermath of the slaughter of the Tutsis, seemed even
more horrendous. And they were. And that was what allowed the fleeing *interahamwe* groups to find cover. They re-organized themselves
within the camps and, with the connivance of President Mobutu, ran
a virtual alternative government just across the border from Rwanda.
And the RPF forces who had by then imposed their control on the
whole country had to endure the thought of their bitter enemies, the
génocidaires, not only enjoying a constant supply of food and weapons
but also attracting the sympathy of the international community. As
Gourevitch puts it: 'through the deft manipulation of mass anguish',
they succeeded in appealing to the world's conscience.

Aid agencies became complicit in this. Under their very eyes, the
Hutu leaders were recruiting and re-arming. The suffering of a million and a half wretched people gave them wonderful cover. This
was the last straw. With France, Belgium, the United States and the
United Nations having played such woeful and even harmful roles
in the tragedy of the Rwandan genocide, the credulity of NGOs and
the humanitarian agencies of the UN offered a grim example of what
Gourevitch calls 'clientitis', too immediate a readiness to embrace
your clients' point of view. Brendan Simms makes the same point in
his analysis of events in Bosnia at roughly the same time. What he
calls the 'humanitarianization' of aid, far from being an attack on aid,
refers rather to a tendency to transform essentially political and strategic problems into humanitarian ones.

When the crisis was finally over and the world started to ask itself
just how it could have stood by while such atrocities took place, politicians too began to address the issues underlying the Rwandan genocide. Bill Richardson, the United States ambassador to the United
Nations, was ready to look the facts in the face. After a meeting with
President Kabila (successor to the dreadful Mobutu who abdicated
in 1997), he acknowledged both the scale of the suffering Zaire and
Rwanda had gone through and the failure of the international community to respond adequately. He was ready to identify the 'climate
of impunity' that had allowed ethnic cleansing to take place and geno-

cidal forces 'to operate, recruit and re-supply' on Zairian territory. And he further acknowledged that widespread killings were continuing. The world community needed to find the balance between stopping the wild assassinations of innocent civilians and protecting legitimate refugees and continuing the work of repatriating them. And all of this should be done without diminishing efforts to bring the genocidal killers to justice.

This wide-eyed and frank recognition of what had happened, the readiness to call a spade a spade, struck a welcome note in what had become a discourse of evasion and subterfuge. It was a statement made by a top-ranking American statesman. It was on the record and delivered in the presence of journalists from some of America's most prestigious newspapers as well as television and radio reporters. Yet not one of them reported it. The indifference of the mass media was yet another nail in Rwanda's coffin.

4

And the Rulers Take Counsel Together

The world has changed profoundly in the last 20 years and continues to do so at a pace frightening to those who grew up in an age of more sedate change. Areas of life that were once clearly and fully governed by national jurisdictions can no longer be dealt with simply on a national basis. In this chapter we look at just six areas of life where national regulation and national responses are totally inadequate to the challenges of our day. Those six areas are not exhaustive but indicators of where we need to have new thinking and new institutional frameworks to harness the positive developments of a globalized world and to control those who would want to subvert those developments for unethical or criminal purposes.

The evolution of global governance will not only mean the 'rulers' taking counsel together but a whole range of networks developing between governments, civil servants, business and the voluntary sector. All this will be breaking new conceptual ground. While the nation state will remain and be a central player in new forms of governance, all the trends indicate that the artificial division of global space into 'us' and 'them', domestic and foreign, will diminish. At a time when 9/11 still casts a long shadow over the world the real challenge will be how governments retain their openness to change and collaborative working and yet address the security concerns.

1 Crime

VAT fraud, cyber crime, people trafficking, gun-running, baby-selling, fraudulent football agents and player transfers, money laundering, drug dealing – organized crime has become big business, big international business. Organized crime bosses have embraced globalization as fully and as enthusiastically as the heads of multinational corporations. National and international policing operations are struggling to keep up with the sophisticated adaptability of the world's crime syndicates.

In the UK alone police are aware of 930 organized crime groups running what is, effectively, a 'multi-billion pound industry'. Drugs are the core business but, as with legitimate business, the criminal gangs soon realize that infrastructure set up to service one type of criminal activity can easily be adapted to others – alcohol, cigarette and people smuggling, for example. Again like big business these domestic criminal gangs, too, form joint ventures with foreign gangs to streamline their operations. As reported by the recently formed UK Serious Organized Crime Agency, 'criminal networks are becoming more fluid, extended and flexible in part due to the use of specialist "service providers" to assist with money laundering, logistics, documents and other enablers' (website of the Serious Organized Crime Agency – www.soca.gov.uk). Things have moved a long way since the Krays dominated crime in the East End of London and met with robust challenges when they moved out of their area – now there is a world without borders for criminality.

A brief look at the operation of two or three of these international crime gangs will give a picture of their range and organization and thus of what the police and other law enforcement agencies are up against. A Netherlands-based gang known as the Verhagen Group had as its 'core business' the importing of cannabis by sea from Morocco, Lebanon and Pakistan and its distribution in Dutch, Danish, British, Belgian and Swiss markets. Their 'peripheral' criminal activities included large-scale fraud and embezzlement, theft of electronic goods, fraud involving precious metals and real estate transactions, and the trafficking of expensive jewellery. There were five known core members of the group but a larger group of associates providing the specialist services. The core members were all Dutch but other members were German, British Asian, African and American. New members were recruited among unemployed persons, students and catering staff but, as with mainstream business, specialist skills were contracted in when required.

The Fuk Ching Gang, composed of about 20 Chinese men from Fujian Province, is based in New York. Their 'core business' is smuggling illegal migrants, human trafficking generally and kidnapping. In New York's Chinatown extortion is their main business. Like other Chinese criminal groups, street gangs like Fuk Ching are affiliated to an organization – in this case the Fukien American Association – which provides a venue to operate from, criminal opportunities and, where necessary, money and guns. Many of the members are also involved in legitimate business activities operating restaurants, shops or taxi services. They have close links with criminal gangs in China and Hong Kong.

A third group, VIS-2, operates in south-east Bulgaria and is involved primarily in insurance scams, illegal gambling and illegal import and export of food, equipment, alcohol and cigarettes. This gang is known to have some political influence at local level, has penetrated into the legal economic sector and has used its power to bring others into its orbit through corruption. This group illustrates how crime can become all-pervasive in countries with weak and corrupt police and law enforcement agencies, in particular the customs service.

This group is typical of gangs operating in Eastern Europe, which tend to use their networks flexibly to indulge in a whole range of illegal activities – counterfeiting, forgery, vehicle theft, smuggling of antiques and cultural artefacts, trafficking of women and children for sexual exploitation and forced labour, and smuggling of firearms and explosives.

Most of the activities carried out by this group take place in the grey area between legitimate and illegitimate business. For example, members act as sponsors for football clubs and openly market their protection services by putting stickers on offices and cars. A recent migrant to Britain from Bulgaria was quoted as saying that her home country 'was not a country with a mafia but a mafia with a country'.

Drug trafficking makes up the largest slice of international organized crime, estimated at around 50 per cent of all illegal activity, and is the most profitable. The profits of the drugs trade, usually in cash, together with profits from all other illegitimate activities can only be utilized if the money can be made to appear as if it were gained from legitimate activity. In other words, this money must not only be put beyond the grasp of asset forfeiture laws but must also be able to re-enter the legitimate economy to buy property or goods or even to finance and run apparently legitimate businesses. This is where money laundering plays its role and where modern developments in the electronic transfer of funds have made it ever more difficult for national and even international authorities to track the complex financial paper trail. It is estimated by the International Monetary Fund that the size of money laundering around the world is around 5 per cent of the world's gross domestic product, or, to put it in more accessible terms, the value of the output of an economy the size of Spain's.

Money launderers exploit the ease, swiftness and sheer quantity of cross-border transactions taking place these days to disguise the origin of their money and move it to places where it is less likely to attract attention – less reputable offshore banking centres and countries with corrupt, weak or non-existent regulatory systems.

As far back as 1989 the seriousness of the problem was recognized by the G8 and the European Union, which together set up the Financial Action Task Force (FATF) to counter the use of financial systems by criminals, to increase collaboration between countries, and to make recommendations to governments about measures to combat the activity. These measures have been further strengthened since 2001 when the fight against terrorist funding was added to the role of FATF. As money launderers have shown themselves to be extremely creative and very flexible in developing new ways to circumvent regulations, FATF and national jurisdictions have to be very nimble-footed to counteract them. Many jurisdictions remain unco-operative with these international regulations and continue to provide a haven for launderers, although Europol has taken on an important role in helping national authorities to co-ordinate their efforts, especially since the advent of the Euro has opened up new possibilities for launderers.

Just as electronic money transfers have made money laundering that much more difficult to combat, 'cyber crime' in general is reputed to be the fastest-growing criminal activity in the world. It includes a whole range of activities – financial scams, computer hacking, credit card fraud, identity theft and bogus websites. Virtual casinos operate in cyber space, often in countries without any form of regulation, so that criminals establish credit using money from illegal activities and then receive a legitimate cheque in exchange. 'Phishing' has now replaced spam as the biggest threat to internet users. It is increasingly the confidence trick of choice for gangs in Eastern Europe, Africa and the Middle East and used to fund crime and even, according to Interpol, terrorism. E-mails, purporting to be from, for example, a bank or an on-line trader, are sent out to people, which lure them into entering their personal details onto sites resembling reputable sites such as banks. Once in possession of those details the criminals plunder the unsuspecting person's accounts with impunity. As some of the sites will only be operative for a few hours, or may 'hop' from one country to another, it makes tracking the culprits very tricky. Legislation takes time to catch up with these new forms of cyber crime so in the meantime companies have to rely on civil actions for trademark or copyright infringement against those who use their logos or straplines illegally.

The internet industry itself (companies, banks, internet service providers, technology vendors and software designers) has taken action in setting up an Anti-Phishing Working Group, putting out a monthly report on sites and also tracking 'crimeware' – software that is introduced onto PCs to detect and steal credentials directly from data held. Nevertheless criminals are usually ahead of the technical game, too.

In recent years combating terrorism has become the major focus for law enforcement agencies around the world. A great deal of the money funnelled to finance Islamic terrorist activity comes from charitable giving. As almsgiving (*zakat*) is an obligation on all Muslims, the volume of charitable giving is immense, and differentiating the legitimate from the criminal is a huge task. In some countries it is only when they experience an attack themselves that they push for tighter domestic controls, as has been the case in Saudi Arabia. In addition the parallel banking system, *hawala*, which operates by personal and family contacts and on the basis of trust or through the use of passwords, means that there is no paper trail to follow for many money transfers.

In the struggle to combat terrorism some commentators point to the fact that states themselves have also become perpetrators of organized illegality, through practices such as internment without trial as in Guantanamo Bay or the 'extraordinary rendition' of suspects to places where forceful techniques can be used to obtain information. These and related activities, which deny people's human rights and restrict their freedoms, are illegal in many countries. In times of heightened criminality and terrorism there will always be a fine balance to be struck. It raises questions about how to maintain open yet secure societies, questions that will need to be repeatedly posed and answered as situations unfold.

People trafficking – especially, but not exclusively, the trafficking of women for the sex trade – is another rapidly expanding area for international crime syndicates. It is a modern form of slavery with up to 180,000 women trafficked from the former Soviet Union into the European Union alone. Women are lured with the promise of jobs or places to study, and in one case a whole dance troupe brought over to perform were lured into the sex trade. It is one of the most globalized trades and so intimidated are the victims that they are used to lure the next wave of women. Up until recently very little was being done to counteract this trade or to deal with the abused women who are its victims. It was only in February 2006 that the British Government signed the Palermo Protocol, a supplement to the Convention Against Organized Crime, which requires countries to introduce criminal offences to combat sex trafficking and to provide assistance for trafficked women. Churches, acting nationally and using their international links, have played a large part in highlighting the plight of trafficked women and in offering them assistance.

With the realization that organized crime is expanding across the world even faster than the more positive impacts of globalization and, moreover, proving a serious threat to security, social and economic development, the United Nations addressed the issue and in September 2003 the UN Convention against Transnational Organized Crime came into force. This Convention urges states to introduce domestic legislation to combat new forms of crime, and to work on new frameworks for mutual assistance between states, on extradition treaties and on co-operating in areas of technical assistance and training. It also assesses and disseminates best practice in combating organized crime. UNODC (UN Office on Drugs and Crime, set up by the Convention) has done regional surveys on two key areas for organized crime, the Central Asian region and West Africa, and has also produced guidance for law enforcers in relation to specific threats, for example, kidnapping for ransom, a rising phenomenon in many areas. As ever these measures can only be effective if states wish to co-operate and have the infrastructure and legislation to be able to do so.

Within the United Kingdom there has been a growing awareness that greater integration of resources and information was needed together with more powers to deal with the growing threat posed by organized crime. So in April 2006 SOCA (the Serious Organized Crime Agency) was formed by the merging of the National Crime Squad, the National Criminal Intelligence Service, the parts of HM Revenue and Customs dealing with drugs and the Immigration authorities for people trafficking. Collaboration with other states is a major part of SOCA's work and only when all states are willing to collaborate, share information and work towards common legislation and enforcement will there be any hope of reining in international organized crime. As long as there are huge differences between countries in employment possibilities, wage levels and standards of living, organized crime will still look like a bright alternative for so many people in the poorer and least stable parts of our world. In the post-9/11 world and as terrorist attacks continue in many areas of the world, there is an added imperative of tackling those aspects of cross-border crime that finance and facilitate terrorism. This is not an insurmountable challenge but one that will require international agreement and collaboration, political will and a creative and proactive use of technology.

2 Environment

In the months and years since the September 11th attacks on New York and Washington, many people around the world, and especially in places where other terrorist attacks have taken place, have come to see such attacks as the greatest threat that humanity faces. Governments in many countries have reacted by pushing through all manner of anti-terrorism legislation and there is scarcely a day when such issues are not covered by the western media.

But there is a convincing case to be made out that the greatest threats to the survival of humankind are not terrorist actions but changes in the earth's environment and their social, economic and political consequences. Attempts to counter terrorism have been tough and speedy, done with selective international co-operation but essentially on a national basis. Efforts to counter the worst effects of environmental change have been tortuous and slow with true international collaboration and consensus difficult to forge, yet such progress is vital to a sustainable future for the earth.

Human beings have had an enormous impact on the planet, especially in the last two to three hundred years: in pouring polluting gases into the atmosphere, in using rivers and the sea as a dumping place for toxic effluent and, in the last century, in moving enough rock and soil to rival the natural processes and movement for the first time in human history. Our planet is a finite entity and so it stands to reason that it does not have infinite capacity to absorb harmful wastes. At the same time 'industrial man' has used up the natural resources that the earth yields at an ever increasing pace. This applies to exploitative use of farm land, where forest cover has been stripped off to open up areas for cultivation. The best-known current example of this is in the Amazon areas of Brazil where vast areas of land have been turned over to soya production and cattle grazing. In stripping such areas of vegetation in this way the local climate is changed and the entire ecosystem of the region brought into jeopardy. The extraction of minerals is another activity through which human beings have left large areas despoiled and of little use for other purposes. If people across the planet are going to be able to move towards a better and more secure lifestyle a new, sustainable approach to the use of the planet's resources has to be found, and found urgently.

Of all the environmental issues facing humanity it is global warming that has received the most attention. Arguments have raged over the years about whether the current levels of global warming are human-induced or part of a natural cycle of constant climatic change. That is really a secondary issue. The fact is that global warming is taking place, and at a faster rate than has been the case during most of human history. Even the most sceptical of observers, such as the Danish statistician Bjørn Lomborg, concede that global warming is an unavoidable fact. The evidence for this is all around us: the shrinking of the ice caps around the poles, the melting of glaciers, and the increase in severe weather events – hurricanes, torrential rains and severe periods of drought. Even the snowfield on the top of Mount Kilimanjaro has almost disappeared, a thing that, from the evidence we have, has probably not been the case for the last 10,000 years. Some Pacific atolls, only a few centimetres above sea-level, have already had to be evacuated and plans made for the gradual relocation of the entire population.

Mark Lynas, in his recent book *High Tide: News from a Warming World*, had this to say about the plight of the Pacific nation of Tuvalu.

I had been in Tuvalu for only two days when the first puddle of water appeared on the side of the small airstrip. More puddles soon joined it . . . Sea-level rise here is a crisis of national survival; very little of Tuvalu is much more than 20 inches above the Pacific and its coral bedrock is so porous that no amount of coastal protection can save it.

Tuvalans will have to move. Tuvalu has recently started legal action to try to win compensation from the countries emitting most greenhouse gases. But how do you put a price on a whole nation being relocated? How do you value a culture which is being wiped out? (Extracted from 'Hot News', an article in *Granta* 83 (Autumn

2003) by Mark Lynas and based on material for *High Tide: News from a Warming World* (London: Flamingo, 2004))

More surprisingly, researchers at the Pentagon have been exercised by the possible implications for US national security of, in their words, 'An Abrupt Climate Change Scenario', and within that report they indicate that 'research suggests that once temperatures rise above some threshold adverse weather conditions could develop rather abruptly'.

They see the results of such an abrupt change being colder conditions in the northern hemisphere. The disruption of the course of the Gulf Stream and considerably warmer conditions in the southern hemisphere will lead to a decline in agricultural production, decreased availability of water, more frequent extreme weather events and subsequent disruption to energy supplies. While this is, on their own admission, a 'worst case scenario', governments around the world have been slow to wake up to the disruptive and costly impacts of the effects of this rapid global climate change. It is salutary to note that it is the insurance and financial sectors of our economies that have done their homework on the impacts of climate change, and their findings are frightening. They report that the costs of extreme weather events have exhibited a dramatic upward trend in recent years. We only need to think of the enormous destruction visited on the southern states of the USA and the Caribbean by hurricanes in recent years. These environmental costs of climate change are rarely factored into the calculations of governments, fearful as they are of disrupting normal economic growth patterns by interventions to mitigate the occurrence and impact of climate change. The effects of climate change in terms of loss of life, destruction of infrastructure and effects on the economy are always greatest in those places that can least afford to deal with them. This poses yet another challenge to the way that richer nations plan for a future sustainable planet.

Scientists from all over the world have carried out a vast amount of research on climate change over the past decades. There is still much work to be done in providing base-line data from which scientists, governments and the business world can work, but the IPCC

(Intergovernmental Panel on Climate Change) has worked to gather peer-reviewed scientific and technical literature and to make that information easily available around the world. It is vital that this work continues and that governments provide the IPCC with all the resources that it needs. Despite the greater availability of information, there are disagreements on detail, yet there is a consensus that climate change is taking place rapidly and that there is a need for urgent and comprehensive action to bring down the levels of emissions into the atmosphere. There is a general agreement that the quality of life for humankind is inextricably bound up with the well-being of the planet. The problem is how to translate this awareness into action by the political and business leaders of the world and into a willingness, on the part of ordinary people, to recognize that their lifestyle choices have an impact not just locally but globally, not just for their generation but for generations to come.

Some of the stumbling blocks in the way of serious international progress on this issue are easy enough to identify. First of all there has been the difficulty in gaining international agreement on climate issues. Getting the Kyoto Protocol ratified proved to be a long-drawn-out struggle. The negotiations have been conducted in the same confrontational context as so many other issues, pitting the developed countries against the developing, the 'North' versus the 'South'. Major players such as the USA have not signed up to Kyoto and there is little chance of their doing so. However, Russia surprised the world by ratifying the Protocol and by doing so has allowed the Protocol's provisions to come into force. While the Kyoto Protocol is an achievement in the current international context, its provisions are too tame. They will scarcely dent the increase in emissions let alone bring the total level of emissions down.

Other ways must be found to gain international consensus that do not depend on nocturnal horse-trading in smoke-filled rooms where for every 'quid' given on one side there is the equivalent 'quo' on the other. Developed nations must accept their responsibility for the historically high levels of emissions. What's more, rapidly industrializing countries such as India, China and Brazil must accept their international obligations to develop in a much more environmentally sensitive way.

Innovative ideas have been brought to the table. Aubrey Meyer's proposals for 'contraction and convergence' have gathered widespread interest and support. His Global Commons Institute has developed this scheme to deal with climate change on a global and equitable basis. It seeks to address the perceived unfairness on which the Kyoto Protocol has been based, namely the locking into place for decades to come of the advantages of the 'haves' and the disadvantages of the 'have-nots' by basing calculations for emissions reductions on levels in the early 1990s.

The global 'contraction and convergence' framework states that climate change is a global problem driven by over-consumption whose impacts are borne unequally around the globe. In order to bring about a reduction in carbon emissions it proposes to allocate the right to emissions on the basis of per capita equal shares. Participating states would fix a long-term target for total greenhouse gas emissions and the necessary cuts required to meet it (contraction). They would then adopt the principle of allocating every person in the world an equal entitlement to emit greenhouse gases by a certain date – perhaps between 2030 and 2050. That objective would then be achieved by graduated steps (convergence). In the transitional period a global market in emissions would transfer resources to poor countries that have surplus emission allowances and force rich countries to drive down their emissions by the technologies being developed for a post-carbon age.

Clearly, for this to work, the reduction in emissions caused by the heaviest polluters will have to be very dramatic indeed. But it is precisely this kind of challenge that a prosperous society is equipped to meet; its capacity to innovate in the market place is its greatest strength. Again, the somewhat sceptical Bjørn Lomborg has calculated that the costs of addressing global warming are not that great; it is essentially imagination and political will that is lacking. It remains to be seen whether a stiffened political will and a heightened level of imagination can be generated to put these 'contract and converge' proposals at the centre of serious discussions at international gatherings.

Only courageous and bold leadership from both the political and the business spheres can really bring about the change of attitude that is needed. This will require change in the way national governments operate and more especially in the way that the United Nations and other multilateral organizations approach their tasks. Already new alliances are being created to work on climate issues – most notably among the world's global cities.

Second, there is the need to overcome the lack of trust between countries of the global South and those of the North. Having had all the benefits of early industrialization in an era when environmental regulation was little or non-existent, richer developed countries now want to burden newly industrializing countries with much more stringent regulation.

All the main international initiatives, both inter-governmental and business, see the route out of poverty for poorer countries to be economic growth, as currently defined, and yet it is unbridled economic growth that threatens the environment through further depletion of resources, massive emissions into the atmosphere and the generation of tons of waste. Any discussion of more environmentally friendly ways of production has to be coupled with a parallel discussion of the plight of the people in poorer parts of the world.

Consumers in the richer world want to enjoy the benefit of cheap fruit and vegetables all year round, of meat from cattle raised on fodder grown on areas of once-forest-covered land in the Amazon, and of flowers flown in from all corners of the globe. These very activities, pursued recklessly for short-term gain, are major contributors to environmental degradation. Moreover, subsistence farmers in many parts of the world struggle to get any living from their soil. They are not environmental vandals. Such people probably have a great sensitivity to the fragility of their land, but they are trying to eke out a living for their families where possibilities are few. Global agreements on aspects of the environment will only be reached and implemented if they address the issues of social and economic development in the poorer countries of the South and in poor regions in the developed world, too. Joined-up thinking is essential if people in the poorer parts of the world are to be given genuine hope for a better and sustainable future.

Third, the behaviour of multilateral business corporations has become a major influence on the international scene. For many campaigners the effect of these corporations is seen as almost totally malign – using up vast amounts of scarce mineral and energy resources, driving down wages by moving to low-cost countries and relocating to areas where environmental legislation is weak or ineffectual. For other people these companies are seen as the major engines of growth for countries that are trying to bring their people out of poverty. Whatever perspective we take these multinationals are a feature of our economic landscape and are here to stay for the foreseeable future. As with all organizations they come in a variety of forms but are neither the devil incarnate nor the solution to all the world's problems. Sometimes, indeed, the activities of international corporations can show better social and environmental awareness than many locally based companies, especially in parts of the world where the enforcement of regulation is weak or ineffectual.

Over the past 20 years business and industry, in the developed world especially, has been subject to greater environmental legislation by the state – the setting of minimum standards for pollution levels into the atmosphere and water courses, for example. Companies that fail to meet the standards are fined or sanctioned in other ways. This approach has been responsible for nudging companies into less polluting ways of production, especially since corporate social responsibility has become a much more prominent feature at company meetings and in the assessment of companies' future performance.

Until recently little emphasis was placed by companies and governments on using pricing and tax signals to encourage the business world into more innovative technologies. Such signals could have accelerated developments in reducing energy consumption, cutting emissions, developing new materials and looking at a lifecycle approach to the production of goods that factors in disposal costs. There also has to be the recognition that 'public goods' – clean air, for example – cannot be parcelled up and sold in the market place and therefore require different and more creative approaches from governments and international bodies.

Significant progress towards more environmentally friendly processes have been made by business and industry – work on low-pollution vehicles, on the development of a whole range of renewable energy technologies, better insulated houses, and more environmentally sensitive town planning. Environmentally driven innovation has the potential for giving businesses the economic cutting edge.

So many of these stumbling blocks could be overcome by education and by the encouragement of consumer power as a major motivator for both government and the private sector to take environmentally friendly production processes and disposal processes more seriously.

It is in the area of climate change and environmental improvement that ordinary people have their greatest power of influence – as voters, as consumers, as investors in companies and as communities taking local initiatives. It is where the paradigm shift for changes in political will and imagination can begin from the bottom up.

3 Finance

Situated as we at Wesley's Chapel are on the edge of the City of London, one cannot but be aware of the feverish activity taking place at the hundreds of thousands of computer screens in the banks and financial institutions that surround us. This is pressurized work, carried out mainly by young people drawn from around the world, which goes on from early morning until late at night and in some places on a 24/7 basis. The potential profits are astronomical (as, indeed are the losses) and the bonuses paid to individual traders often in the six-figure bracket. Yet the casualties are high: burnt-out, disillusioned workers, banks and companies initiating or being the victim of predatory take-overs, and the unseen effects of much of this speculative activity being worked out on unsuspecting people just trying to earn a living in their own countries all around the world.

The internationalization of financial activity over the last 20 years is probably the single most dramatic illustration of globalization. The sheer scale of activity is massive with the concurrent development of technology allowing the electronic transfer of funds, which has meant that vast flows of money circle the world at the touch of a button. All this has been made possible by the relaxing of foreign exchange controls, the deregulation of interest rates, the removal of credit controls, and the opening up of a huge range of investment possibilities to foreign investors. It feels as if the global financial markets have taken on a life of their own, using their own opaque language and disconnected from normal daily economic life – and this is precisely what has happened.

In this context it is salutary to remind ourselves that money – in whatever form – is a medium of exchange, a standard unit of value and a store of wealth, but that money is not an end in itself but merely a means to an end – the development and flourishing of human society. Trade and industry, the provision of education, health and welfare services, are what human society needs and what money can help facilitate.

The sheer scale of transactions in the global finance markets is astounding and they completely dwarf those of the so-called 'real' economy of manufacture, communications, transport, etc. US$15 million were daily traded worldwide on average in foreign exchange dealings in 1973 but by 1998 that had risen to US$1,490 billion per day. The current level is a little lower than that but still in the 'stratosphere'. To put this in more understandable terms, it takes the wholesale foreign exchange markets just a month to trade the value of annual world Gross Domestic Product (GDP).

The global trade in money and its associated forms has grown, many would maintain, out of all proportion to the needs of the economy and society – the financial system has become disconnected from the real world. What we have, in effect, is a financial supermarket in cyber space with investors 'betting' on future commodity prices and currency rates. At its worst this activity can result in high volatility and rampant competition, with global speculators taking advantage of weak regulation to make profits in 'emerging markets'.

Even if governments, individually or collectively, wanted to rein in and regulate this activity it is becoming less and less possible for them to do so because the activity of multinational or transnational corporations rivals that of nation states. Another aspect of globalization has been the great increase in these companies – up to around 50,000 by 2000. Out of the 100 largest economies in the world, 51 are corporations and 49 countries. As the headquarters of these companies are located in a restricted number of countries – North America, Europe, Japan and South Korea – their activity adds yet another element of asymmetry to the North/South wealth divide.

The liberalization/deregulation orthodoxy that the International Monetary Fund (IMF) and the World Bank had been advocating since the 1970s received some rude shocks in the 1980s and 1990s that came close to putting the smooth working of the entire global financial system into jeopardy. A closer look at the Asian financial crisis of 1997–8 will illustrate some of the problems.

The East Asian economies of Japan, China, Hong Kong, Singapore, Indonesia, Thailand, South Korea and Malaysia experienced 30 years of pretty solid growth from the 1960s. By the mid-1990s banks around the world were eager to lend into these Asian markets and foreign investors were anxious to get a slice of the emerging markets' profit potential. So a great deal of money poured into the region – often of a very short-term and speculative nature. Companies over-borrowed, asset prices soared and pressure to further liberalize economies was not accompanied by similar efforts to ensure proper supervision and regulation. When the global economy suffered a downturn in 1996 it brought an abrupt end to the high export growth rates of a number of these East Asian 'tiger economies', especially those supplying computer parts. Thailand was the first country where the asset bubble burst. A combination of incompetent government, imprudent borrowing and inflexible exchange rates put pressure on the Thai currency and it was forced to devalue – unleashing a flood of bad debts and setting off a contagion that spread throughout the region. Capital flowed out of the region faster than it had flowed in. For five countries – Indonesia, Malaysia, Philippines, South Korea and Thailand – private capital flows reversed from an inflow of $97 billion in 1996 to an out-flow of $12 billion in 1997. Thailand's currency, the *baht*, came under relentless pressure and reluctantly the government had to call on the International Monetary Fund to bail it out, but the shock of the collapse of the *baht* led to a crisis of confidence in the other currencies of the region. What happened was like a gigantic bank-run on the whole of East Asia. The crisis showed the tremendous volatility of the global financial markets. The close linkages between the Japanese economy and the economies of the rest of East Asia meant that very quickly this local panic could run out of control and become a worldwide crisis.

While the investment community and the international financial institutions looked for ways to stem the contagion, ordinary people in the region were reduced from relative prosperity to near abject poverty almost overnight. Despite the loss of face involved, Indonesia and South Korea, as well as Thailand, all had to ask for help from the IMF. The economic hardship politicized the populations, leading them not only to criticize their own governments for over-speedy liberalization but also to turn against the foreigners whose short-term speculative activity had played such a large part in the humiliation of their economies. More damaging were the claims that the IMF in applying stringent conditions as part of its response to the crisis was, in fact, promoting the interests of its main contributors (western nations) above the interests of East Asian countries and their people.

The East Asian crisis and subsequent ones in Russia and Latin America have prompted calls for reform from within the global banking and investment community. At the same time ordinary people have taken to the streets outside the meetings of the IMF and World Bank, the Davos World Economic Forum and the meetings of the World Trade Organization to demand globalization with a human face.

The question of exchange rates between currencies is critical. International trade encourages the use of freely convertible currency but many countries have tried to peg their currencies to the US$ or to a basket of major currencies. In a world of instantaneous electronic transactions this has proved very unwise. In 1997 the Thai authorities wasted most of their foreign reserves trying to shore up the *baht* before finally having to give in to devaluation, a scenario familiar in Britain in relation to Black Wednesday in 1992, when the UK was forced to withdraw sterling from the European Exchange Rate mechanism (ERM). Foreign Exchange spot transactions amount to US$ trillions per day, and although less than 5 per cent of it is actually related to trade in goods and services this vast speculative activity can cause serious damage to business and to the economic stability of countries. The economist James Tobin has put forward a proposal for a small tax of around 0.1 per cent on all such transactions, which would reduce the worst speculative excesses and also yield funds for development purposes. A similar idea was proposed by Keynes in the 1930s but, although it has gained the support of some prominent people, it is still regarded as unworkable and there seems to be little real will at the international level to push for it.

The financial crises of recent years have highlighted once again the absence of any effective mechanism for burden-sharing between debt-or and creditor nations. The plight of highly indebted poor countries has been kept before the world's eyes for decades by campaigning groups and yet, despite many initiatives and good intentions, many countries of the global South are still paying back interest on loans granted in the heady days of the 1970s oil boom. Creditor nations are able to negotiate stringent terms for the rescheduling of payments. This is in sharp contrast with a normal commercial situation in which the credit-giving financial institution shares in the loss should the borrowing company get into difficulties or become bankrupt. Proposals for an international insolvency procedure have yet to gather any serious head of steam, because of the perception that countries cannot be 'bankrupt'.

It is now over 50 years since the Bretton Woods institutions – the IMF and the World Bank – were set up. They were designed for a very different context – the reconstruction of Europe after the Second World War. They developed when sovereign states were the only significant actors on the world stage and each institution had a limited mandate to deal with a very specific area of concern. Although they have tried to be flexible in extending their mandate outside Europe, their governance, practice and guiding principles are still very much tied to their origin in the northern industrialized world.

In the absence of an independent reserve currency, the US$, accepted virtually everywhere, functions as such. This gives an enormous advantage to the USA which can print money at almost no cost to itself while it has to be borrowed at high cost by poor countries. Replacing the US$ with a neutral reserve currency would introduce an element of equity into relations between richer and poorer countries. However, as with the UN Security Council and its five permanent members, so with the US hold on international currency dealings – nothing much will change until those with the power see that it may well be in their best, long-term interests to collaborate and seek a way forward in which the interests of all the world's people can better be met.

Another problematic aspect of the current massive movement of funds around the world is the existence of offshore (and onshore) financial centres – around 60 in number and increasing – where depositors are offered low taxation and high confidentiality. These offshore centres hold vast amounts of money in deposits that escape the normal taxation regimes and are undeclared in the owner's country of residence. It has been estimated that the annual tax revenue lost is somewhere in the region of US$255 billion. This is effectively a global subsidy to the corporations, which can choose to domicile their headquarters in such centres, and to the wealthiest people in the world – the so-called 'hinwis' (high net worth individuals) beloved of the offshore banks.

Globalization has progressively undermined the territoriality principle on which traditional tax regimes are based. As ever it is the poorer developing countries whose revenue collection systems are least able to cope with the changing situation and whose wealthy citizens enjoy the privilege of capital flight to offshore havens. It is only recently, with the urgent need to put a stop to money laundering and the movement of funds by terrorist groups, that bank secrecy has begun to be overridden. Again it is interesting to note that exchange of information between governments about capital flight was urged on the architects of the Bretton Woods institutions way back in 1944 but came to nought as it was opposed by the USA, a major beneficiary of capital flight.

So, as in so many other areas, the governance of global finance and its regulation needs to develop to meet the needs of the time. At present it is too diffuse and unco-ordinated, with governments, inter-governmental bodies and regulatory bodies from within the financial world all developing their own responses to meet the demands of the time but largely in an ad hoc and unco-ordinated manner. There are developments within the banking world overseen by the Basle Committee on Banking Supervision, which in 1997 produced a set of core principles for effective banking. There is the increasingly important Financial Action Task Force, set up in 1989 by the Central Bank Governors of the 10 most important banks together with 24 of their southern counterparts and the Finance Ministers of the G7 (8). This in turn has led to the setting up of the Financial Stability Forum to enhance the exchange of information and the level of co-operation between states in the surveillance of commercial financial institutions. Each area of financial dealing has its own regulatory body, for securities, for insurance, for accounting – a veritable proliferation of acronyms representing groups whose existence and remit remains largely unknown to the world at large. In this the financial sector presents an outstanding example of a major trend in contemporary governance – the growth of non-official mechanisms of regulation. The weakness of the position is that there are no universally applicable laws governing financial services and that weak and failing states do not participate in the current regulatory systems and often have little capacity or will to do so.

So the major concerns for global governance of the world of finance remain: data deficits in many areas; limited competition in some sectors leading to excess profits and lack of consumer protection; concerns about the efficiency of overlapping and unco-ordinated bodies; the volatility of the global markets; and, of greatest concern, the divorce of finance from the 'real' economy.

One brighter spot on the horizon has been the European Union where there has been a deepening of integration in the financial sector through a progressive harmonization of standards and regulations. The European Monetary Union and the European Central Bank exemplify ways in which closer integration brings with it the demand for stronger international governance, which in turn leads to yet further integration. It may be that this is a route ahead for other regional groupings to follow. Large questions still remain about how huge economies such as that of China are to be integrated not only into the global financial sector but into its governance mechanisms also.

In the world of global finance largely unaccountable technocrats hold sway to an extent found in few other areas of contemporary governance, and this leads to a narrowness of vision, secrecy, the continued dominance of those who were there first (the northern industrialized nations), and immunity from democratic scrutiny. There are no votes in financial regulation; most MPs and ministers do not have a clue and are not interested, and this is true across the world. This must change if the interests of the people of the world are to be met, not just the interests of the rich elites.

4 Health

For hundreds of years most diseases were specific to and confined within particular geographical regions. Malaria and most parasitic infections, for example, were confined to tropical regions while diseases like measles were a temperate speciality.

The colonizing movement of people from the developed world to Australia and New Zealand, North America and South Africa carried unfamiliar diseases to these parts which resulted in huge numbers of the indigenous populations dying through lack of any immunity to diseases common elsewhere. There was also a reverse process in which large numbers of colonial civil servants and missionaries died of tropical diseases to which they had no resistance. The institutes and hospitals for tropical diseases that exist in the countries of the North are a legacy from this period and still provide some of the best care and research in connection with illnesses of this kind.

The transmission of communicable diseases has always blurred the health 'frontier' and made governments aware that, in matters of health, political boundaries are no barrier to the spread of infection. In the fourteenth century the Black Death killed around a third of the population of Europe, and in the early twentieth century the global spread of the influenza epidemic killed more people than the casualties of the First World War.

But these days, as a result of migration, travel, tourism and climate change, diseases of all descriptions are spreading freely around the world. The number of international travellers has tripled since 1980 and now runs at over 3 million people each and every day. So what is new is, to use a recently coined phrase, 'the scale of microbial traffic'. Old and new diseases, viruses and infections in both animals and humans are spreading not only further but faster and putting national and international health surveillance mechanisms under severe stress. Diseases of poverty and diseases of affluence, from the tropics and the temperate regions, all have a global reach and impact now.

As in every other aspect of our life on this globalized planet, the advances in medical science in the rich world stand in stark contrast to the dire situation of people in the poorer world who still die in their millions through diseases of insanitation, through easily preventable infections and through the effects of hunger. So while the richer countries of the North ponder how to deal with an ever-ageing population who take up an increasing share of the health facilities in their old age, countries and areas in the poorer world still face high levels of maternal and infant mortality, deaths from preventable diseases and generally low levels of public health.

In previous generations in Britain people's health was improved most dramatically through the provision of clean water and better sanitation, though vaccination and better basic nutrition. The better-off saw it as in their interests that the 'lower orders' became healthier and thus a much reduced threat to their own health and well-being. Philanthropy and fellow human feeling coincided with a realistic and pragmatic self-interest. In our highly mobile world this understanding has now to be translated onto the world stage. The health provisions at the heart of the Millennium Development Goals, with their targeted efforts to deal with TB, HIV/Aids and malaria, show one possible way ahead. These Development Goals emphasized the link between the basic alleviation of poverty, the provision of water and sanitation, improved nutrition and the achievement of better health provision for the people of the poorer parts of our world.

But bridging the gap between health provision in the low and high income countries is no mean challenge. Many poor countries now face multiple challenges and the poorer they are, the less able they are to face these challenges. Continuing high rates of population growth in many countries mean a growing demand for health and social services. In sub-Saharan African countries, for example, resources have had to be diverted from basic health care to dealing with the HIV/Aids pandemic. Just as more health-care professionals are being trained greater numbers have been lost both through becoming HIV infected themselves and because of the skills-drain as large numbers of doctors and nurses leave to staff the hospitals of the countries of the North.

The pursuit of improved health should be a cause that unites all human beings. In birth and sickness, recovery, care and ultimately in death all people find their common humanity. In our world of violence, mistrust and division, the issue of human health and well-being should constitute an aspiration that commands willing support across the world. Yet, as in so much else in our world, the gulf between the health 'haves' and 'have-nots' is vast, growing and complex.

Specific international initiatives are addressing some of these major problems and making a positive and significant impact. As is so often the case, many of the most impressive are little known. GAVI – the Global Alliance for Vaccines and Immunization – brings together the private and the public sectors to improve the provision of vaccines to children around the world. The range of collaborating partners offers one model for effective engagement with primary health issues on a global scale. GAVI brings together governments in developing and industrialized countries, established and emerging vaccine manufacturers, non-governmental organizations, research institutes, UNICEF, the World Health Organization (WHO), the Gates Foundation and the World Bank.

Another impressive initiative, Drugs for Neglected Diseases, grew out of the work of Médecins sans Frontières, as they recognized the lack of effective drugs for dealing with some of the most widespread infections in the regions where they worked. The most neglected diseases – sleeping sickness, Chagas disease, leishmaniasis and Buruli ulcer – are parasitic infections that are pretty well confined to poor people in poor countries. Such people are too poor ever to constitute a market that can attract commercial pharmaceutical companies into drug research and development. Some of the drugs currently in use for treatment of these diseases are 70 years old, have very serious side effects and are becoming less effective because resistance to them has now developed.

These two recent initiatives and many others indicate an increased awareness on the part of governments, foundations, non-governmental organizations and pharmaceutical companies that relying on purely economic mechanisms cannot solve the problem of improving public health in low-income countries. Market mechanisms to drive research and innovation in developed countries just do not work in places where there is no effective market for drugs because both government and the population are too poor to be able to buy such products. For companies it is far more profitable to invest in drugs that deal with male sexual dysfunction than in those that could contribute to stemming the explosion in drug-resistant malaria. Intellectual property rights and patents, which act as incentives to the pharmaceutical companies in their development of new drugs and diagnostic techniques in the rich nations, are irrelevant to conditions in low income countries where there is not only poverty but a complete lack of infrastructure to support new drug development. The HIV/Aids pandemic has brought these two worlds together. It has exposed the ethical dilemma of how to respond to the enormous need for drugs in countries that are poor while not undermining the role of patents in commercial research and drug development programmes in the rich world.

Widely divergent pricing by the main pharmaceutical companies for the same product in different countries puts into question their current pricing practices. It highlights a lack of transparency with regard to the relationship between product costs and pricing. Generic drugs have been produced, for example in India, at much lower prices but this development is resisted by the pharmaceutical companies except in 'emergency situations' – a concept still vague and undefined.

Matters of patents and intellectual property rights generally are at the heart of the work of the World Trade Organization. In 2001 in Doha, under pressure from those who wanted to make drugs, especially those for treating HIV/Aids, more easily accessible to populations in low income countries, there was a move to ensure that intellectual property rights be interpreted in a manner supportive of public health. There is little evidence so far that this has freed up the production and trade in such drugs.

Whether it is initiatives for coping with HIV/Aids or malaria, effective child immunization or treatment for TB in developing countries, all are dependent on the provision of accessible health-care facilities and more especially on the availability of trained medical personnel. Here we meet another serious problem of our globalized society: the migration of health personnel – doctors and nurses particularly – to the developed world. This brain drain is haemorrhaging scarce medically trained manpower from the South to the North. For example, figures from a recent WHO Report show that for every 100 doctors working in sub-Saharan Africa, 23 African-trained doctors are working in the countries of the OECD (Organization for Economic Co-operation and Development). The contrast between the position in the Americas and that in sub-Saharan Africa is stark: both areas have about 12 per cent of the world's population but the Americas have 42 per cent of the world's health workers while sub-Saharan Africa has a mere 3 per cent.

In a number of middle income countries with good medical education facilities – Mauritius and the Philippines, for example – a proportion of students are trained specifically to be able to migrate to richer countries, earn a good income and send remittances home. For these people, and for others who are part of a planned programme, overseas experience has the positive element of further training. But for most countries of the South the flight of their trained human resources means the loss of a return on their educational investment and effectively a donation to the wealthy countries to which their people have migrated. So serious is this issue and so damaging to better health provision in a whole swathe of countries that it now appears high up the agenda of all international health meetings.

Globalization of health issues brings other challenges, too. In most countries there are restrictions on access to drugs but there is no consistency of practice from country to country. Indeed, one country's policy and its public health management may be subverted when a neighbouring country allows unrestricted purchases of drugs. The growing trade in pharmaceutical products on the internet is another way in which national authorities are bypassed and regulation breaks down. All manner of bogus and counterfeit drugs – from the useless to the dangerous – are offered for sale. Sick people dissatisfied with the advice and treatment they have received from their own health services or desperate for a cure for a terminal illness will stop at nothing in their search for a wonder drug or treatment. Costly and unproven stem cell treatment has been offered to people with degenerative diseases over the internet, which when investigated revealed an international black market in umbilical cord stem cells.

A whole new form of tourism has arisen from much the same motivations – people 'shopping around', usually through the internet, for the cheapest treatments or the shortest waiting times. In Britain the NHS has had to recognize this to an extent, as in cases where it has paid for hip replacement operations done in France, but the long-term implications of this trend pose many serious questions in a world where the funding and structure of public health systems are so different. In our globalized world people search the world for what they want and medical tourism is one area that is booming. Holiday packages exist that combine a trip to the Taj Mahal or a yoga holiday with heart bypass treatment in one of India's specialized private health facilities. Germany is the place of choice for cataract treatment, Hungary for dental work and South Africa for cosmetic surgery. As ever the difficulty is in assessing the credentials of the health facility overseas and the question of who picks up the costs and the 'repairs' when things go wrong. New legislation in Britain on the disclosure of the identities of sperm and egg donors has led to a decline in donations in Britain and the development of 'fertility tourism'. Taking advantage of cheap flights, childless British couples are travelling to Spain, Cyprus and Eastern Europe for their fertility treatment. The other side of this development is the trade in eggs and sperm, with adverts for donors, and specifically tall fair-haired and fair-skinned ones, appearing in the Polish and Russian press. As some countries seek to regulate fertility clinics and protect both donors and recipients the free market plays out in much of the rest of the world, and with it the criminal fringe, making money out of trade in the organs of poor people and the desperation of sick or infertile people.

With the internet at the centre of so much of the global market in health and welfare and all the problems to which that gives rise, it is easy to forget the positive potential of such technology. Up until recently patient and doctor usually needed to be in close proximity. People in remote areas and in poor countries suffered serious disadvantage. Now telemedicine allows investigation, monitoring and management of patients at a distance. This could redress some of the inequalities caused by the migration of health personnel to high income countries and cities; again it poses a challenge to the world to bridge the technological gulf between the low and high income countries. Telemedicine points the way to a future when physical distance may no longer be a barrier to health care as long as we can bridge the digital divide and work towards providing information and opportunities for shared learning across the world; for information as a global public good accessible to all.

First it was SARS (Severe Acute Respiratory Syndrome) in 2003, then came the threat from bird flu. Both of these have posed the question as to what extent global health governance is equal to the task of dealing with infections with such potentially global impact. Traditionally the World Health Organization has acted in health matters in much the same way as the Security Council has acted in matters of conflict – mediating between consenting countries and not interfering in the internal affairs of a country. The spread of HIV/Aids and TB around the world brought a higher political profile to health issues and also began a revolution in global disease control – an awareness that governments alone cannot deal with such threats and a move towards increasing the powers of the WHO in relation to states in the context of infectious diseases. This trend has continued as the WHO has faced the need to combat SARS. In the context of increased possibilities for bio-terrorism it is important that these gains in global governance be sustained. On the one side will be the challenge of finance. The Global HIV/Aids Fund, a practical demonstration of the collaboration of governments, private sector companies and non-governmental organizations, has struggled to get adequate funding – states have been dragging their feet and failing to live up to their fund pledges. What will be the attitude of states faced with the next infectious disease crisis if they are unable or unwilling to finance the current ones? On the other side will be the willingness of states to put global needs above their own national interests. Some states have already begun to question aspects of the WHO's travel advisory powers. Those close to the development of global health governance see the next few years as being critical in the effort to sustain and consolidate the gains that have been made: nothing less, in fact than a seminal challenge for twenty-first-century humanity.

Migration and travel, food standards and environmental conditions, internet use and misuse, the role of the state and the role of non-state actors, private and public partnerships are all critical for a holistic approach to matters of health in a globalized world. In matters of health the personal and the political meet – a common ground, a place for shared security – if only effective global mechanisms can be forged.

5 The Media

At the time of the invasion of Kosovo journalists were on board the ship that launched the first rocket, and an American reporter took a photograph of the rocket as it soared away from the vessel towards its target on land. He linked up his computer and sent the image to his editor in the office in New York, who was able to print the image and get the paper out on the streets and onto its website before the missile had actually hit its target.

Again we recall that, at the time of the bombings of 7 July 2005, the first images on our screens came from the mobile phone cameras of ordinary people caught up in the tragic events.

The last 30 years have seen enormous changes affecting all forms of media and the pace of change of 'space-shrinking technologies' is still accelerating. Powerful communications technologies have not only changed the pace and capability of the media but their role, too. From being reporters of news, opinion-formers, advertisers and purveyors of a predominantly western mass culture, the media, especially the electronic media, have become participants and actors in the very news they purvey.

From the 1970s onwards technological, political, legal and regulatory changes, part of the general trend towards the liberalization and deregulation of economies, have transformed the media scene around the world, especially in the core areas of the wealthy world. The digitalization of information has allowed a great expansion in the number of TV channels in comparison to the restricted possibilities of terrestrial channels. Coupled with this has been the development of satellite and cable technology, opening up a whole new range of broadcasting possibilities including the internationalization of many broadcasting channels.

The use of satellite technology has made distance irrelevant for the broadcaster and has allowed programming to be beamed to a large number of places simultaneously. While the first wave of technological innovation impacted largely on the developed countries of the world where people had the money to install the costly technology, subsequent waves have rolled out over much greater areas of the world. The take-up of satellite services has been greatly enlarged by the link-up with cable networks, which has allowed subscribers to receive a wide range of channels themselves without the need to invest in expensive reception hardware.

Deregulation and economic liberalization over recent years have also facilitated the trends within the media that have now become commonplace in many parts of the world. The first is a concentration of ownership of the media, to the extent that 20–30 multinational corporations dominate the entire scene. Second is the shift from public to private ownership, with public broadcasters like the BBC becoming endangered species. Third, there has been a growth in the transnational structure of many of the media conglomerates, all based in the wealthy northern countries with America far out in the lead. AOL/ Time Warner, for example, has television channels, production companies, magazines, films, music labels and the internet. Other American multimedia giants include Disney, Viacom, General Electric and News Corporation. Fourth, with a lowering of the regulation criteria on cross-media ownership, corporate diversification and mergers have increased between telecommunications companies, the producers of film and TV in both satellite and cable form, and more recently computer based communication, as can be seen in the list of global media empires already referred to. Vast empires have come into being that control a nexus of media, entertainment and information provision (what Benjamin Barber calls the 'infotainment telesector'), dominating the 'production' of news and spreading addictive TV shows and the advertising that goes with them, all around the world.

Hotels in virtually every big city in the world supply CNN to their rooms. Even in some of the remotest parts of the world satellite dishes receive such stations and put out public showings in towns and villages in much the same way as people once gathered around the one radio in the neighbourhood.

The quality of much of the output from these media empires is questionable: long-running soap operas, reality shows, the making and breaking of 'personalities', acres of advertising. Interspersed among all of this is some news, preferably the sort of news that gives spectacular 'visuals' – scenes of war and natural disaster, of accidents and violence. And all of this is beamed into countries with widely differing cultures and widely differing understandings of the images they see. At one and the same time people in more traditional societies are shocked at the moral standards purveyed on the television and in the films and yet they are attracted by the goods that they see advertised and aspire to the lifestyle of America. The proliferation of global music, movies, tapes and videos is particularly attractive to the young generation and has given rise to a global culture where teenagers around the world have more in common with each other than they do with their own parental generation.

It is the American-based media that are most active in syndicating or broadcasting their output all around the world, and that can be damaging enough to local language, culture and custom in other countries, but the impact of their output at home is perhaps more damaging.

The US domestic media are intensely parochial, inward-looking and self-absorbed, as any visitor from outside experiences who tries to tune into a radio channel that gives international news and fails to find one. Radio programmes are banal and filled with advertising and local trivia. TV channels really only venture outside the USA to report major disasters or American-led initiatives – most often of the military kind.

Americans are allowed, even encouraged, to live with the myth that America is the world and the world is America. The media work to keep American people closed to experience from outside and ideas that are current in the rest of the world. This has very serious political implications for it means that the people of the world's most powerful nation are shielded from knowledge and debate about the consequences of their country's engagement with the rest of the world. Most of the programming is aimed at the 'advertising-desirable' stratum of society and the lobbying power of the media mega operators makes regulating in favour of a more balanced output a very tough assignment. Against this background it is not surprising that the general American reaction to the bombings of September 2001 was, 'Why do people hate America so?' And this is what passes as the vaunted 'free press', a virtual TV universe where people in the USA and around the world live in a fantasy world of soap operas, quizzes and personality shows, which is often more real than the world outside their front door.

Who regulates all of this? To whom are the media moguls account-able for the material that they disseminate? What national or interna-tional legal provisions are available when satellites are broadcasting from space and beaming their wares into a range of countries, unfet-tered by constraints of local culture or norms? Some observers have termed the present situation 'electronic colonialism', in which poorer nations are in a dependent relationship to the post-industrial devel-oped nations and in danger of having their own language, norms, values and expectations swamped by foreign norms and expectations. The inexorable march of the English language (American style) con-tinues apace through the output of the global media giants.

Whereas old-style colonialism sought to control the land, resourc-es and labour of the colonized, in the age of electronic colonialism it is control of the mind that is now being sought as desires, attitudes, lifestyles and consumer behaviour are moulded to a largely North American pattern.

It is not in the least bit surprising that there have been reactions to this 'electronic colonialism'. Some of these reactions could be termed 'constructive' while some are clearly negative and potentially danger-ous. In the 'constructive' category we might put Al Jazeera and other satellite channels that have sprung up around the world giving a region-al viewpoint on current affairs. In the negative and dangerous category we can note the reaction of many in Muslim and other traditional soci-eties who react in extreme and even violent ways against what is per-ceived as the moral laxity of what is purveyed on western media.

In the mid-1990s the BBC established an Arabic language satel-lite television service, Al Jazeera, but dumped it when their Saudi Arabian partner pulled out. Al Jazeera is now financed by the Emir of Qatar from a base in Doha. It is the most watched channel by the millions of Arabs living in the Middle East and around the world. It has presented one of the rare challenges to the dominance of the Eng-lish language satellite stations and has encouraged the development of a number of other similar channels, including one pro-American station, Al Hurra, financed from the US but singularly unsuccessful in winning its target audience.

Al Jazeera has tried to move away from its financial dependency on the Emir of Qatar but has found advertising revenue difficult to secure. Nevertheless it has developed an English language service, and dedicated business and documentary channels and websites – in Arabic in 2001 and in English in 2003. *The Economist* recently commented that 'satellite television (Al Jazeera and the other Arabic channels) has created a sense of belonging to and participation in, a kind of virtual Arab metropolis'.

It has begun to make real a dream that 50 years of politicians' speeches and gestures have failed to achieve: 'Arab unity'. The implications of that should give concerned observers of the world scene pause for some considerable thought.

It is interesting to see how western attitudes to Al Jazeera have shifted over time, from alleged attempts by the Bush government to blow up the station to western political leaders, like Britain's Tony Blair, seeking to use the station to air their views. The station has gradually earned respect for its balance and relative independence. Al Jazeera wears, as a badge of honour, the fact that it has been censored and censured as much by the governments of Arab countries as by western nations.

The lesson of Al Jazeera has not been lost on other parts of the world. Plans have been proposed for an African equivalent of Al Jazeera; the bankroller has yet to be found.

As finance and technology have allowed the development of challenges (such as Al Jazeera) to western and predominantly US saturation of world news and media provision, so that same technology has allowed the development of a more 'grass-roots', bottom-up form of journalism. The internet, the rise of 'blogging', chat-rooms and the ability of the on-line media to combine still and moving pictures, sound and text mean that across the world individuals can become news creators as well as news consumers. As the media giants try to extend their control and range so what one commentator describes as the 'vibrating din of small voices' extends across the globe.

This was most spectacularly illustrated by Matt Drudge, the one-man-internet-band who was responsible for broadcasting the

Clinton–Lewinsky story across the world in 1998. Undoubtedly the story would have surfaced through the more usual press channels but Drudge picked up the story and with the push of one button put it out across cyber space, precipitating a scramble by established reporters and news agencies to get follow-up stories. For many in the media business this became a defining moment, illustrating the impact of the internet and the power that it gives to individuals. Drudge himself commented that 'every citizen can now be a reporter, can take on the powers-that-be', and he included the media in that category, too. Is this now where the 'free press' is to be found and are there any constraints on the innumerable 'bloggers' out there? 'Blogging' permits anyone, virtually anywhere, to establish a personal diary or a pulpit to the world. There is no professional code of conduct, no Press Council or watchdog holding them to account – only their individual conscience.

If Matt Drudge, his fellow-travellers and the bloggers of the world carry the torch for democracy and freedom in the cyber world, there is then, also, the far darker side to the internet's possibilities. We have already seen the use of the internet by extremists – disseminating dangerous ideas, whipping up emotions and orchestrating demonstrations around the world. Governments, not least in Britain, are aware that they do not have the ability to monitor fully, let alone censor, the internet.

This brings us to the thorny issue of regulation of the media both on a national and international level, and especially of how to develop a regime of international governance that will make efforts to bridge the existing digital divides and ensure that internet expansion can be done in the orderly manner that is so crucial to its yielding benefits to all its users.

As in most other arenas, the struggle is between the USA with its cutting-edge technological advantage, the rest of the developed world, and the peripheral nations who have most to gain from being able to use electronic communication and media. Domain names and internet protocols are at the heart of orderly expansion at present. In 1998 the US Department of Commerce set up ICANN (the Internet Corporation for Assigned Names and Numbers), a private entity given a gatekeeper role over developments. There were challenges to this body, from within the USA on grounds that it was monopolistic and from without on grounds that it was not sufficiently global in its governance, although it did have an international Board of Directors. Naturally there are calls for a shift from a US-based ruling entity to a multilateral one, and this is something being pursued through the controversial WSIS (World Summit on the Information Society).

Here is not only a dilemma for the global community and its future communication and media needs but also supremely for the USA itself. For the economic well-being of the USA itself is crucially dependent upon an orderly bridging of the world digital divide so that all countries can be brought within the new 'information society'.

The ITU (International Telecommunications Union) is one of the great success stories of the UN – so successful that we never think to comment on the miracle of being able to place a telephone call between any two telephones anywhere in the world. From time to time the USA has threatened to pull out of the ITU as it pulled out of UNESCO during the height of the Cold War struggle over the New World International Communication Order (NWICO), but the ITU is not only central to the future of international telecommunications but also central to the development and thriving of the global economy – from which, for the time being at least, the USA is the largest net beneficiary. Currently the USA is very conscious of the threats and opportunities posed to its position by the economic growth of China. It is chilling to note how the internet service providers based in the USA, such as Google and Yahoo, have been willing to provide the Chinese government with internet filtering technology. This allows the self-censoring of their websites and search-engines at the behest of the government.

Since September 2001 the attitude of governments all around the world towards the internet has changed. While measures have been introduced to deal with the propagation of terrorism as well as to combat child porn and cyber crime more generally, the development of surveillance and filtering techniques has allowed countries to deal with many other 'inconvenient' aspects of the internet.

What a shame that the second leg of the recent World Summit on the Information Society was held in Tunisia, a country that vies with China for top of the league in suppression of the press and freedom of expression. Yet some progress was registered there with a 'lightweight' forum established to discuss internet governance while oversight was left in the hands of ICANN and the US government.

As the struggle continues to maximize the benefits of electronic communication across the globe while dealing with its threats and dangers, the role of the individual 'media consumer' could well receive more attention. As 'pollution of information' is an ever-present threat for ordinary people trying to make sense of their lives, far more attention needs to be given to the media education of people across the world. Given the huge impact of the media upon us much more attention needs to be given to helping people discern that impact and develop critical tools with which to deal with all forms of media output. It is the consumers in the end who will determine what survives and what dies in the media jungle.

6 Migration

Migration – the flow of people from one part of the earth to another – has been a fact of life from the beginning of human history. It is a constant and not an aberration in the story of human societies. People have travelled along rivers, crossed over seas, scaled mountain ranges and penetrated forests in search of new lands for agriculture, new resources to exploit, new peoples for conquest, space to get away from oppressive 'others' or a search for freedom and the possibilities of a better life. Migrants have often been among the most dynamic and entrepreneurial members of society.

Over the last few hundred years there have been huge movements of people: vast numbers shipped from Africa across the Atlantic to America and the Caribbean as slaves; early settlers in their hundreds of thousands leaving Europe for Canada, America, Australia, New Zealand and South Africa; Asians moving to Africa and the Pacific to work on plantations; people moving from the Iberian Peninsula to the countries of South America. The peopling of our world has been as much a story of movement as of natural population growth. So why, in this era of globalization, has 'migration' become such a huge, difficult and often contentious issue?

While there may be much disagreement about what constitutes 'globalization', how new a phenomenon it is and how 'global' its reach is, there is consensus around the definition of globalization as a movement towards greater interdependence and integration among the nations of the world. Globalization is seen in increased trade, vast financial flows across the world, instantaneous electronic communication – in a nutshell, in life lived across national boundaries. Advocates of globalization welcome 'free flows' across borders – in almost everything except people. Yet one of the most noticeable effects of globalization has been its uneven spread and the growing disparities in standards of living within and between countries – hence the increased trend in migration. It is in the issue of migration that economics and ethics collide; in the issue of migration the bluff of the globalizers is called more clearly than anywhere else; in the issue of migration the fall-out from 9/11 has been felt very strongly as security fears have been focused on the 'foreigners' in our midst.

It is estimated that approximately 175 million people, less than 3 per cent of the world's population, currently move across borders to live for longer than a year. Far more people migrate within their own countries – from small villages to towns and then to large cities in search of employment and the chances of a better life for themselves and their children. Movement within countries responds to a large extent to market forces: people move to where they can get work, or to where the work is better paid. Migration across borders is also subject to market forces but as one of the most defining characteristics of national sovereignty is the right to exclude – to decide who comes in and who stays out, who can become a citizen and who cannot – market forces co-exist uneasily with quotas and controls and, of course, the evasion of those controls.

When the economies of European countries picked up after the Second World War huge numbers of 'guest workers' came in on a variety of terms to provide labour for the burgeoning economies – Turks and Kurds to Germany, people from French-speaking North Africa to France, people from Indonesia to Holland and people from the Caribbean and later parts of Asia into Britain. When, in the wake of the oil price increases of the 1970s, European economies went into tailspin and the 'guest workers' were no longer needed, even the most authoritarian governments could not bring themselves to send their 'guest workers' back although in many instances they had the right to do so under the arrangements negotiated at the time of their recruitment. As the Swiss novelist Max Frisch commented at the time, 'we imported workers and got people instead'.

With increasing globalization in the 1980s and 1990s the flows of people across national borders have become greater in size and much more diverse in both their source and destination countries. Human mobility has become an integral part of the global economy in which companies and countries look further and further afield for workers who can fill their jobs and contribute to their competitiveness.

Latest estimates on migration flows from the Global Commission of International Migration are interesting. (It is in the nature of the case that the figures will usually be underestimates.) The USA is the most significant host country with some 35 million migrants, 20 per cent of the world's total, and is followed by Russia, Ukraine and India each with between 6 and 8 million. Other significant migrations are between neighbouring countries – Zimbabwe to South Africa, Egypt to Jordan, Burkina Faso to Côte d'Ivoire, Indonesia to Malaysia and Haiti to the Dominican Republic. A number of countries, while having much lower numbers, have very high percentages of migrants: Andorra, Macao, Monaco, Qatar and the United Arab Emirates all have over 60 per cent. China (35 million), India (20 million) and the Philippines (7 million) are the most important source countries. Overall the number of migrants has doubled in the last 25 years. However, migrants now depart from, transit through and arrive in almost every country in the world; the old distinctions of countries of origin, transit and destination are now increasingly difficult to sustain.

Migrants' economic contribution to their host countries is very significant but their contributions to their countries of origin are even more astounding: formal remittances were worth about US$150 billion in 2004 with perhaps double that amount being transferred informally, providing a much more significant contribution to the economy of many countries than official development aid. None of these figures takes into account the large and growing 'irregular migration' and the money made by those who exploit such migrants – thought to be in the region of US$10 billion per annum.

In analysing migration, the problems it throws up and the opportunities it offers, it is helpful to distinguish different types of migration. There is movement of people between rich or middle income countries, which usually involves professional people moving with their transnational company or international organization as part of their career advancement. There is movement between poor countries, which is often linked to employment possibilities or as the first step on a migration to a richer country. Whereas the migrations of the nineteenth and twentieth centuries were from the old world to the new, much of the migration is now from the poor to the rich world – from Mexico to the USA, from the countries of Anglophone Africa to Britain, Canada and the USA, from Francophone Africa to France, from the countries of Asia and the Pacific to Australia and New Zealand. These flows carry within them seeds of discord while at the same time alleviating the problems of ageing societies, especially in Europe.

Some migrants are unskilled and some skilled. The skilled make up for shortfalls in various professions in the rich world – doctors, nurses and IT experts, for example – and may cause a brain-drain situation for their country of origin. For example, in the UK in 2003 one third of the doctors and 10 per cent of the nurses were foreign-born, according to an Institute for Public Policy Research (IPPR) survey entitled *Migration and Health in the UK*. The unskilled fill lowly jobs in richer countries – cleaners, drivers, security guards, construction workers, filling station attendants or domestics. They relieve the unemployment situation in their home country and, with the skilled, often remit a great deal of very welcome foreign exchange to families at home.

Some of the migration flows are the result of negotiations between countries and have clearly defined conditions, some countries, as mooted for the United Kingdom, employing a points system as the basis for letting in foreign workers; but the numbers of people wanting to migrate for work from poor countries exceeds the normal legal allocations and so people resort to a host of illegal means to get to their desired destination. 'People smugglers' take advantage of these conditions, charging huge sums to 'smuggle' people into destination countries. A whole 'migration industry' has grown up.

In a world of huge discrepancies between the wealth of countries and of the level of wages paid, not to mention the differences in foreign exchange rates of differing currencies, enterprising people will always seek a better life for themselves and their families. Students sent to study abroad by their government, company or family with the intention of returning home are often attracted by employment possibilities and stay on after the termination of their studies – legally or otherwise. The availability of information and the possibilities of relatively easy travel enable potential migrants to have a global perspective when they think of moving, yet the most potent factor in determining the direction of migration is the existence of networks of family and friends – so any flow from one country to another is likely to trigger further flows.

In Europe, the USA and Japan and other rich-world countries businesses look at migration from another perspective and one that often puts them at odds with their own governments. In those places there are ageing populations and those of working age are not eager to do jobs that are dirty, dangerous or have unsocial hours. Firms, therefore, have a real incentive to use migrant labour, people who can be paid less and who generally speaking do their job with more zeal and a willingness to work longer hours. Once jobs become 'migrant jobs' they tend to remain so with migrants from new source areas coming in to fill the gaps left by the upwardly mobile participants from the previous wave of migration. Migrant labour helps firms in the richer world to compete with lower wage economies and to resist the need to move their whole operation to lower wage countries.

The success of the British economy and those like it has been built on casual migrant labour, much of it sub-contracted for maximum flexibility to labour agencies, or gangmasters as they are more commonly known. This workforce can be turned on and off or diverted from one activity to another at a few hours' notice. Companies using agencies and gangmasters, including suppliers to many of the major supermarket chains, claim that they make every effort to comply with immigration procedures and employment legislation, but the system is rife with allegations of exploitation and illegality. Migrant workers themselves tell a very different story – of the absence of any employment contract, delayed payment of wages, no breaks, unpaid overtime and constant bullying.

Another strategy businesses use in the pursuit of lower costs, usually referred to euphemistically as 'competitiveness', is to outsource their work in cases where technology allows services to be provided without having to locate the producers/providers and the consumers/ users in the same place. We are now used to an Indian voice on the line when we, in Britain phone our bank for account details or try to book an airline ticket, but in parts of the USA this outsourcing has gone further than that. There are old people in residential homes in New York and other American cities who carry beepers on which a person from India rings to remind them that it is now time to take their medicine! But many, many services cannot be provided unless the providers and the users are in close proximity – so the demand for migrant workers will increase, not least in those very same homes for elderly people all around the rich world.

The potential and the problems of migrant labour are felt most in the cities of our world and especially in the global cities – New York, Tokyo, São Paulo and Johannesburg, but most noticeably in London, perhaps the most global of the world's global cities.

It is not without significance that it is in cities like London and New York that migrants – irregular, undocumented, illegal – are beginning to assert their claims for a proper recognition of their presence, their vital contribution to the economy and their need for proper conditions of work. For example, while most of their members are not citizens of the United Kingdom, the London Citizens Workers Association campaigns for a living wage for the capital's 'hidden workforce'. Likewise in the USA illegal Hispanic workers are asserting their rights to recognition for the vital role they play in the US economy.

The challenge for global cities, for nations and for the international community is how to regulate migration in such a way that the benefits that accrue from it are maximized and difficulties and threats minimized. As with so much in our globalized world the difficulty standing in the way of better international agreement, regulation and monitoring of migration is the asymmetry between the position of rich countries and poor countries.

Rich country governments are moving towards policies that favour the immigration of skilled workers and discourage unskilled migrants, while poor countries have an interest in their unskilled and often unemployed workers getting work overseas and sending remittances to help family members at home. Poor countries, on the other hand, are not eager for highly trained and skilled people to leave, except where some protocol can be negotiated to allow such people to work in an overseas country for a fixed period and receive some additional training as part of the package. Restrictions in richer countries on the immigration of unskilled workers, especially in cases where employers want to hire such people, feeds illegal immigration, floods of asylum claims and the burgeoning industry in smuggling and trafficking of people.

Much of the present legislation in countries across the world fails all those who have a stake in migration issues. It fails those who want to enter a foreign country for work and the citizens who do not want illegal migrants. It fails employers looking for workers to fill jobs and governments seeking to reduce crime related to people smuggling and trafficking. It fails governments seeking to maximize revenue and reduce costs related to bureaucracy and deportation.

The year 2000 saw migration appearing high up the agenda of many international organizations – the World Bank, the United Nations High Commission for Refugees, the World Trade Organization. This was in sharp contrast to the situation just a decade earlier when calls for a conference on migration coming from the United Nations fell on deaf ears and was rejected by migrant-receiving countries for fear that such a conference would entail yet another bruising North/South confrontation. It was clear then that migration was escaping the control of even the most capable of rich country governments. The idea that global governance of international migration was vital was still viewed as an intrusion on national sovereignty.

As the movement of people across the world is so dynamic and continuously evolving to meet new challenges and new opportunities perhaps a seismic shift is required in the way these issues are conceptualized. Even the term 'migration' may need to be rethought – a global mobility regime is what is needed, which can encompass non-state actors, deal with the phenomenon of transnational communities of people who have a foot in two if not more worlds, and recognize the importance of remittances and the training that people can receive out of their own country.

Whatever forms of governance emerge they need to be able to deal with the criminal elements in the migration business – people smuggling, trafficking, passport manufacture, deaths in transit – and to ensure proper conditions for workers across borders in countries other than their own. The task is huge and the penalties for not establishing collaborative procedures will be increased strife between migrants and host communities.

5

How Long, O Lord, How Long?

We've been arguing that we live in a world whose main mechanisms for problem-solving or conflict-resolution are grounded firmly in conventions that honour state sovereignty and the inviolability of boundaries. At the same time, a global culture is emerging where most of the shaping influences that affect our everyday lives cross those same boundaries with impunity. It should, therefore, be obvious that we need urgently to face some important questions. Where exactly do we go from here?

First of all, we should be honest about the limitations of current methodologies. It's simply not enough to stretch available theories or traditions to make them fit every emerging crisis. New wine won't always go into old wineskins. Christian thinking at this point would do well to recall the readiness, shown within Scripture itself, to go on looking at past events (even those central and most cherished in the tradition) with a readiness, sometimes a radical readiness, to abandon old ways of interpreting them in favour of an entirely fresh consideration. Clinging to the particularities of one's own history, or to a particular moment in one's own history, seems bound to lead to tears. There is a dignity in difference but that cannot be a reason for turning what differentiates us into absolutes. There must be dialogue and open-ness; we must learn how to listen and act; our resolve in this area is likely to be tested by our readiness to invest the capital of our diverse traditions in a future whose shape we can neither foresee nor control. In other words, this is a time for faith.

The challenge to religion

Richard Dawkins has been a strident critic of religious belief for many years. He is lionized by the press and his polemic fuels a debate that often has more heat than light. His latest book *The God Delusion* turns his hatred of religion into a 'crusade' (a word chosen with deliberate irony!). In his view, religions have brought the world to the very brink of chaos and, if not checked, could push us into an apocalyptic scenario of truly horrific proportions.

People of faith should avoid the twin temptations of either ignoring Dawkins or simply going onto the defensive. There may be more behind his criticisms than meets the eye. His emotive outbursts and undoubted brilliance of mind lead him into picaresque joustings with those he loves to pillory. But, at least in some respects, he may be nearer the truth than religious believers like to imagine. Just a few minutes looking at the thinking of Christian fundamentalists, for example, might persuade us that there may be circumstances where people of broadly based faith positions should consider making common cause with humanists and secularists. Together they might seek ways to subvert the ideology of those who not only seem to believe in an apocalyptic end-time scenario but are also working with great commitment to make it come about.

The beliefs of these fundamentalists are shaped by a literalistic understanding of the Bible and a readiness to apply its meaning uncritically and anachronistically to the events of our own day. Convinced that the second coming of Christ is at hand, and knowing it will not come about until all the biblical prophecies relating to such a moment have come to pass, they have developed an end-time vision of genocidal battles that envisage the Jews in full possession of the Holy Land. Then, and only then, will Christ come. The faithful will be snatched up into rapture and the Antichrist will massacre the unfaithful (including unbaptized Jews). Christ will defeat the 'enemy from the north' and institute his millennium of peace.

This apocalyptic vision has widespread currency among many evangelical groups on both sides of the Atlantic. It leads its adherents into an uncritical support of the state of Israel, not out of a desire for the ultimate well-being of Israeli citizens but because of the expectation of an end-time event in which a strong Israel will play its part. This is not a merely theoretical (or marginal) construct. It is impossible, for example, to gauge how much it shaped the responses of those wielding power as the Israeli armed forces unleashed their weaponry and technology on southern Lebanon in the summer of 2006. While this was happening, we heard America's political leaders referring to Syria and Iran as if they were the very embodiment of the description 'enemy from the north'. The marriage of minds on these matters and the perfidious and incalculable influence of fundamentalist Christian thinking on the political establishment of the USA make for uncomfortable reflection. The dangers are only too obvious. Thinkers of this kind identify a whole list of contemporary questions – homosexuality, divorce, single parenthood, abortion, stem cell research – as evidence of a social disintegration suggesting that we are indeed in the end-time. There is no need to worry ourselves about global warming or indeed global needs since God is about to put his own strategy into play. The end is nigh.

This would be laughable if it weren't so serious. Dawkins may be right. This is highly dangerous thinking especially if, as many believe, it materially (or even sub-consciously) affects the thinking of politicians. Why else would President Bush veto the Stem Cell Research Enforcement Act, for example, a course of action almost unheard of for a legislative proposal previously endorsed by both Houses of Congress? And why exactly has the USA defiantly refused to sign up to the Kyoto accords on global warming? And what is the explanation for America's innate suspicion of the United Nations?

Nor are these fundamentalists merely a way-out bunch of deluded idiots. The advice given by the Roman Catholic bishops of the USA to their members ahead of the last presidential elections shows an overlap with the fundamentalist agenda. Catholics were advised that it would be wrong to cast their vote for anyone whose stance on issues like homosexuality, abortion and stem cell research wasn't in line with official church teaching. Boiled down, this amounted to the Roman

Catholic bishops endorsing the Methodist President Bush's candidature and opposing the Roman Catholic John Kerry!

These internal contradictions within the Christian community ought to be set alongside attitudes towards dialogue with other faiths where the fault lines are not difficult to discern. Pope Benedict XVI got into all kinds of trouble in his address to the University of Regensburg in September 2006. He quoted a fourteenth-century Byzantine emperor's unflattering description of the prophet Muhammad: 'Show me just what Muhammad brought that was new and you will only find evil and inhuman things such as his command to spread the faith with the sword.' Efforts to make this seem a 'storm in a teacup' remain unconvincing. As do attempts to blame the press. The Pope did, after all, have quite a record on questions relating to Islam. In 1986, the then Cardinal Ratzinger refused to attend Pope John Paul II's landmark inter-religious prayer gathering at Assisi, which included a high-level Muslim delegation. He expressed himself fearful lest people misinterpret his presence as an endorsement of syncretism and religious relativism. In 1998, he publicly criticized a document on inter-religious prayer. Two years later the Congregation for the Doctrine of the Faith, which he headed up at the time, issued *Dominus Iesus*, subtitled 'On the Unicity and Salvific Universality of Jesus Christ and the Church', a document that was widely disliked because of its alleged triumphalism and insensitivity to other faith traditions. Islam was on a list of religions described as 'deficient'. Later, just before his election, he stated in an interview for the French newspaper *Le Figaro* that he opposed Turkey's entry to the European Union on the grounds that that predominantly Muslim country was 'in permanent contrast with Europe'. Such an assessment seems conveniently to forget the considerable contribution of Islamic culture and learning to the shaping of modern Europe. Shortly after becoming Pope, he held a private meeting with Oriana Fallaci, an Italian writer and journalist known for her strong critique of Muslim immigration to Europe. All this suggests unease on the part of the Pope on this and related matters. He has made serious efforts subsequent to the demonstrations that followed his Regensburg address to repair the damage. He has initiated conversations with Muslim leaders to improve relations and continued with his visit to Turkey even when many thought he might be better advised to cancel it. But these gestures are unlikely to alter the basic consideration, namely that the Roman Catholic Church finds it intrinsically difficult to entertain the idea that Islam's religious and theological claims might merit serious attention.

Pope Benedict's erstwhile friend and fellow-theologian, Hans Küng, has taken Christian thinking in a quite different direction. He's set out his concerns quite simply:

- There can be no ongoing human society without a world ethic for the nations.
- There can be no peace among the nations without peace among the religions.
- There can be no peace among the religions without dialogue between the religions.

Küng's readiness to test all his previous positions is truly remarkable. It began with the radical questions he put to his own Roman Catholic Church in such books as *Infallible?* (1970) and *The Church Maintained in Truth* (1979). This was a careful reconsideration of what Küng called 'the Counter-Reformation Church' and was the fruit of the thinking he'd done through the time of the Second Vatican Council. This was enough to lose Küng his licence to teach in Roman Catholic theological faculties, a high price to pay for his efforts.

He went on to establish a ground-breaking agenda for Christians in general. *On Being a Christian* (1974), *Does God Exist?* (1978) and *Eternal Life* (1982) put a thoughtful and truly ecumenical theological framework at the disposal of many people. Indeed, they were best-sellers. His ecumenical pilgrimage took him into ever-widening areas, first into the realms of inter-faith dialogue and then into his concerns with global responsibility. No one has maintained the dignity of difference more than he – he remains a faithful Roman Catholic priest – but nor has anyone recognized more than he the importance of taking one's secure identity into a wider world of dialogue and mutual encouragement.

As Christians engage in such dialogue, they must be prepared to look critically at some of the biblical material they've previously used as the basis for their universalist claims. And here, no one has been braver or more challenging than Kenneth Cracknell whose book *In Good and Generous Faith: Christian Responses to Religious Pluralism* (Epworth, 2005) should be required reading for anyone interested in this agenda. In five chapters, he traces a salvation history, a Christology, an ethic, a spirituality and a missiology 'for Religious Pluralism'. He addresses texts like 'No-one comes to the Father but by me' (John 14.6) in an inclusive way without, in our view, sacrificing his intellectual integrity. And the note that resounds throughout the volume is that it is indeed possible to contemplate a world where people of different backgrounds and faiths can live together (rather than apart) and offer the dignity which emanates from all that differentiates them to the search for harmony and peace. This is not only possible but desirable. And not only desirable but necessary and urgent.

The challenge to theories of the just war

The tradition of the possibility of a 'just war' has been developed over many centuries. Its roots are in the teaching of Augustine in the fifth century and it has passed through the thinking of Thomas Aquinas with a number of refinements along the way. The tradition was fashioned within the Holy Roman Empire and was intended to help decide how to regulate the regular outbursts of hostility between Christian states. The criteria that emerged assumed the common values and allegiances shared between the combatants.

There have always been two main areas for consideration within this tradition. The *jus ad bellum* defined the main questions to be looked at before the outbreak of conflict. Who has the right to authorize the war? Has a just cause been established? Are the intentions of those moving into hostilities appropriate? The *jus in bello* group of questions come into operation once a war has begun. The first of these relates to the need to ensure immunity for non-combatants. The other deals with proportionality and gives attention to methods of limiting or restraining the use of force so that it is appropriate to the case in question. There is a clear recognition within every version of this theory that the use of force should always be a last resort.

It doesn't take long to look at the disputes and wars we've outlined in our third chapter with these questions in mind. Let's take the *jus ad bellum* questions first. Who authorized these hostilities? The United States intervened in Bosnia after much prevarication on the part of NATO and the European Union. Indonesia sought to overwhelm East Timor and incorporate it into its own territory despite repeated appeals and resolutions from the United Nations. It was a people's liberation struggle in Eritrea but no one could have been blind to the massive military strength of an Ethiopian army equipped by both the Americans and the Russians. Haiti saw its legitimate government overthrown by a military junta while the world looked on indifferently. Iraq seems a case apart. Opinion varies, even there, between those who believe there was a legal basis for intervention (the unfinished business of the 1991 war) and those who thought a second resolution of the UN Security Council was needed. As for Rwanda, the Hutu *interahamwe* forces simply did as they pleased. By whose authority did these conflicts take place? By the whim of those with interests to defend or establish. And the international community? On the whole, useless.

Was there a just cause for these outbreaks? Ethnic cleansing in Bosnia demanded some kind of response. Large-scale massacres of its population and the naked imperial aims of its enemy made the defence of East Timor a moral imperative. In Eritrea, a country that had been sacrificed to its powerful neighbour, it was obvious that annexation by Ethiopia could only occur by brute force and against the clear determination of its population. Haiti had received fulsome promises from its continental neighbours that a military coup d'état would not be tolerated. Whatever opinion one holds about the Iraq war, no one can doubt that Saddam Hussein's treatment of the Shi'a Muslims, Marsh Arabs and Kurdish populations made some kind of action necessary. And it was genocide in Rwanda that declared its own imperative.

Were there right intentions? Could Serbian militarism and ethnic cleansing ever be called a right intention? Could Indonesian or Ethiopian imperialism be justified in this way? What about the intentions of the military junta in Haiti or Saddam Hussein's tyranny in Iraq? Is the question of right intentions even relevant when genocide takes place as in Rwanda?

Do the *jus in bello* questions fare any better? Certainly not. Once conflict has broken out there seems increasing readiness to abandon the conventions that bound opposing sides in former times. Civilian populations are routinely the victims of violence. Indiscriminate use of weaponry has led to untold thousands of deaths in the conflicts we've described in earlier chapters. Genocide and ethnic cleansing, suicide bombs and guerrilla tactics, economic sanctions and blockades, ill-directed rockets and the use of cluster bombs, the use of human shields and hostage-taking, torture and arbitrary executions – all have played their part. As indeed have the activities of regular armies deployed in an overly muscular way. In case after case, little or no attention seems to have been given to the interests of non-combatants. They have been sacrificed by the thousand and the hundred thousand.

The use of force has not always seemed a last resort. Often it has had more to do with opportunism or troop readiness or naked greed. And it has rarely been used proportionately. The machetes of Rwanda and the technology of modern armies have all been deployed with devastating effect. Local disputes have become international disasters. East Timor lost a third of its population before the world community took an active interest in its affairs. Appeals were constantly made to either a just war tradition or the tenets of international law but sometimes it's felt that these were just stalling mechanisms. While diplomats and lawyers talked, many of them under the direct aegis of the United Nations, untold numbers were being killed. No one can doubt that there are times when the UN, almost alone, can bring opposing camps together for negotiation and debate. It has, again and again, shown just how vital it is in the present state of the world. And yet the atrocities continue. This inevitably raises the question whether the UN is a 'toothless tiger'.

Charles Jones, Reader in International Relations in the Centre of

International Studies in Cambridge, offers a different approach to these matters in his 'War Within Reason: Not Just War', written for the July 2006 number of *Cambridge*. He argues that the just war tradition is not at all helpful in today's world. It was useful when the monarchs of France, England, Spain and other European countries were steadily establishing sovereign authority over consolidated territories at the expense of Pope and Emperor. The scholastic theologians of the time attempted to formulate a doctrine of how armed conflict between sovereigns could be contained within the moral realm. Jones asks searching questions.

> Where does legitimate authority reside in a world where many states have long since lost control of large tracts of their territory and armed groups flourish without any clear political programme or aspiration to secession or control of the state while permanent alliances or regional unions such as NATO or the European Union begin to acquire a measure of autonomy, even from their most powerful members, and uncertainty about the authority of the UN Security Council is aggravated by the pretensions of the United States to a quasi-imperial regulatory role?

Christian thought about moral issues, he argues, has always been more concerned with intention than outcome and war is no exception. And this leads him to describe the difficulty that follows from 'the grounding of contemporary thought about war in Christianity'. And to ask whether the tradition can be successfully secularized.

The importance of such an exercise is, once again, to see whether it may be possible to establish a 'global ethic' where 'some substitute for the divine authority that was once held to underpin political authority' may be identified. Jones quotes Michael Walzer at this point. In his *Just and Unjust Wars* (acknowledged by Jones as 'the most enduring secular contribution to the tradition') the author declares the inevitability of 'privileging the state of which one is a citizen' as the corner stone for the evolution of such a tradition. And yet, as we have been insisting throughout the pages of this book, arguments based on the sovereignty of the state (and therefore from mere national interest) have actually fed many of the disputes we've been considering. Secular thinkers face a second problem too, argues Jones. They must work out how to strike a balance between intentions and outcomes. As Jones puts it:

> Recall Augustine's maxim: 'Love, and do what you will!' If a Christian accepts this injunction, consequences are thereby subordinated to virtue. Even war may be undertaken in a spirit of love. For the non-believer, by contrast, consequences may seem to be just about all there is, and certainly not lightly to be disregarded. Conversely, there is no Lord to know the secrets of our hearts. Once again, separation of the tradition from its implicit theology poses problems.

For many Christians, of course, all talk of a just war is unacceptable. War can never be justified, certainly not from the viewpoint of Christian theology. For others, the assessment of whether a particular dispute could amount to a just war is a box-ticking exercise. Once again, it seems that Hans Küng gets near the mark. The new world order, in his view, cannot be realized on the basis of 'realpolitik' (in the manner of Richelieu, Bismarck, Palmerston or Kissinger), 'a mere ethics of success'. Nor on the basis of 'idealpolitik' (as with President Woodrow Wilson at Versailles), 'a mere conviction ethics'. What is needed, according to Küng, is 'an ethic or responsibility which presupposes a moral conviction, but realistically seeks the predictable consequences of a particular policy'. This will need an art of politics that combines sharp political calculation with a well-reflected ethical judgement and a broader understanding of 'self-interest' in a globalized world.

Clearly, there is a desperate need for our philosophers, political theorists, international lawyers and (yes) theologians from all the major faiths to work at an acceptable framework that can give us appropriate conceptual tools to work with.

The challenge to our international institutions

The major international and multilateral institutions with which we are working in this new millennium are ones that were set up in the last millennium and in response to the issues of that time. So, we have the United Nations, the Bretton Woods twins – the World Bank and the International Monetary Fund – and the World Trade Organization. The World Trade Organization is a development of the General Agreement on Tariffs and Trade (GATT), which itself was the watered-down version of the International Trade Organization vetoed by the USA but intended to be part of the post-war settlement.

All those institutions, the creation of the victorious powers of the Second World War, were designed primarily to rebuild Europe and to avoid another economic depression by ensuring the economic stability of the world. These institutions actually aimed at ensuring a relative autonomy for national states from global forces. Enshrined in these institutions were mechanisms that entrenched the power of the world's most powerful nations and effectively institutionalized the wartime alliance. The Security Council, the major part of the UN system for dealing with breaches of international peace and security, gave the power of veto to the five main nations, the USA, USSR, France, Britain and China, as the price for having them 'on board'. The development of the multilateral mechanisms of the UN was stunted by the emergence of the Cold War stand-off and the competitive struggle to recruit newly independent nations into one camp or the other.

The end of the Cold War ushered in a brief moment of euphoria and raised expectations in which people looked forward to a new world order of peace and economic development. How naïve we now see that to have been. The UN and other multilateral bodies could not be expected to deliver on those raised expectations without radical reform.

The post-Cold War world was now a very different place. The UN and its agencies were challenged to adapt to the new era in which membership now totalled 191 states with very different levels of development, different hopes and different expectations of what the UN could and should deliver for them. The first crisis of the new era was the break-up of Yugoslavia and the bloody conflicts that ensued in the Balkans. Little did people imagine that there would be a bloody ethnic conflict in the heart of Europe nor how ill prepared the UN, EU and NATO would be to deal with it.

One of the key foundations upon which the UN had been built was the principle of non-interference in the internal affairs of sovereign states. Article 2/7 of the UN Charter states that 'nothing contained in the present Charter shall authorize the United Nations to intervene in matters which are essentially within the domestic jurisdiction of any state'. What, then, was to be done when states fell apart? How was the world community to react when states or parts of states waged war on their own people or failed to protect them? Was the international community just to stand by and watch as ethnic groups were targeted for being wiped off the face of the earth?

Although the principle of territorial integrity and political independence was enshrined in the UN Charter as quoted above there was an 'escape clause' – 'but this principle shall not prejudice the application of enforcement measures under Chapter VII'. Chapter VII deals with 'action with respect to threats to the peace, breaches of the peace and acts of aggression'. The UN has struggled to bring Chapter VII into effective operation and, as we have seen, has been slow or ineffective when situations demanded decisive intervention. Even where the Permanent Five members of the Security Council have managed to be in agreement, for example over the North Korean nuclear test in 2006, there has been a reluctance to invoke Chapter VII of the Charter.

The changed geo-political reality at the end of the second millennium begged yet more fundamental questions about state sovereignty. The only 'authority' higher than the state that had been recognized at the time of the Westphalian solution (the recognition of the sovereignty and equality of nation states at the end of the Thirty Years War (1618–48) in Europe) had been the higher norms of religiously inspired 'natural law'. With the secularization of Europe and the end of the Catholic Church's claim to a territorial empire the 'natural law' theory fell away. Yet an essentially seventeenth-century European notion of state sovereignty was enshrined and given universal applicability in the founding document of the United Nations. It is usually forgotten that for long periods in the history of our world the 'national' was not 'normal' – it took serious work to make society 'national'. As Saskia Sassen has stated, 'there was nothing natural, easy or predestined about the national'. One commentator has argued that the entrenching of state sovereignty in international relations reflected 'organized hypocrisy'. Only recently, under pressure of events, has it been possible for a dialogue to begin about the acceptability of intervening in the affairs of states against their wishes. This has been felt most sharply in places where the state has unleashed violence against sections of its own population – in East Timor, Rwanda, and in the former Yugoslavia.

Here there is a challenge to Christians and people of other faiths who have 'universalistic' claims to work together to help make 'internationalism' as normal and natural as a world based on the national came to be for earlier generations.

While at the practical level the UN has to deal with how the international community intervenes to stop deaths by intent or neglect within member countries, the reformers of this body have had to try to break out of the old conceptual frameworks and point the world towards an evolution in global governance that will move beyond the nation state and embrace the role of a whole range of non-state actors.

At the same time the UN has to take on board what individual states are reluctantly recognizing, namely that in so many areas of life national governments no longer have the control they once had. We have seen how the mobility of people, the development of technology and the speed of communication mean that our world has moved a long way along the spectrum from an international society of separate states towards a global web of political, social and economic interdependencies.

All this is being played out in the aftermath of the events of 9/11 and in the context of the war in Iraq. It is inevitable that these events cast a huge shadow over our contemporary world and have caused 'security issues' to rise to the top of the agenda of 'northern' nations. For all that, we would do well to step back a little, try to assess the state of the world through eyes that are not American, European or British, and take care that we do not define the future or develop governance structures based on these considerations alone.

At the same time, there is also a growing recognition that the 'market' alone cannot take care of everything. Governments of nation states are actually being called upon to take an enhanced role, not least in some security-related areas such as the clampdown on money laundering and the financing of terrorist activities. It is governments that are being asked by the Financial Action Task Force to freeze the assets of suspected terrorists. So the existence of 'failed' or weak states, places where the writ of the government does not run to cover the whole territory, is just as threatening to the peace and stability of the world as places where there is open violence and repression within states.

How can the current multilateral institutions, especially the UN and its agencies, adapt to meet the challenges of our times? A great deal of very helpful thinking has already been done over the last few years. In 2001 the International Commission on Intervention and State Sovereignty produced a ground-breaking report, *The Responsibility to Protect*. In it there are clear connections with the speech that Prime Minister Blair made in Chicago in 1999 in connection with the intervention in Kosovo.

At the core of the responsibility to protect are two basic principles. The first is that state sovereignty implies responsibility and the prime responsibility for any state is the protection of its people. Second, where the population is suffering serious harm as a result of internal war, insurgency, repression or state failure and the state in question is unwilling or unable to halt or avert it, the principle of non-intervention yields to the international responsibility to protect.

This report identifies three aspects of the state's responsibility to protect: to prevent, to react and to rebuild. It is interesting to note the emphasis on rebuilding where it points up the necessity, particularly after military intervention, to provide full assistance with recovery, reconstruction and reconciliation and an addressing of the root causes of the initial conflict. There is also a stress on the long-term nature of much rebuilding of society and infrastructure. The principles for military intervention set out in the report follow closely the 'just war' criteria mentioned earlier in this chapter.

The drafters of this report, many with long international experience, recognize that it has often been impossible to ensure a Security Council resolution to allow an intervention for humanitarian purposes. They propose alternative options in such a situation – either that the matter be referred to the General Assembly under the 'Uniting for Peace' procedure or that action will be taken by regional groupings in the area of concern subject to authorization by the Security Council. (The 'Uniting for Peace' Resolution was introduced by the United States in 1950 during the Korean War as a way of allowing the General Assembly of the UN to act when the Security Council is paralysed by the use of the veto.)

Importantly, the report states,

> the Security Council should take into account that if it fails to discharge its responsibility to protect in conscience-shocking situations crying out for action, concerned states may not rule out other means to meet the gravity and urgency of the situation – and that the stature and credibility of the United Nations may suffer thereby.

In 2004 the UN Secretary General, Kofi Annan, convened a high-level panel on threats, challenges and change entitled 'A more secure world: Our shared responsibility'. The report of this group, issued in 2005, affirms many of the recommendations of *The Responsibility to Protect* but adds other more specific recommendations related to the UN and its agencies. It proposes a definition of terrorism as

> any action . . . that is intended to cause death or serious bodily harm to civilians and non-combatants, when the purpose of such an act, by its nature or context, is to intimidate a population, or to compel a government or an international organization to do or abstain from doing any act.

The high-level panel also came up with some recommendations on the reform of the UN system, namely the establishment of a Peace-building Commission in place of the Trustee Council and the Military Staff Council. The main functions of the Commission would be identifying countries that are under stress and risk sliding towards state collapse and with the national government planning assistance to try to prevent collapse. It would also have a role in planning for transitions between conflict and post-conflict peacebuilding over whatever period may be deemed necessary.

The report also acknowledged the need for an expansion of the Security Council to 24 members and offered two models based on a regional distribution of seats.

Everyone who has studied the United Nations and its operations is clear that there is need for reform. Equally it is acknowledged how difficult, if not impossible, it will be to get the current privileged Permanent Five to concede significant power and control. To approach reform in this top-down structured way is perhaps not the most productive route for progress.

The first challenge to UN reformers is the need to acknowledge that the UN cannot do everything that all its member countries would like it to do. This was always true but now the demands outweigh the resources more than ever. The UN is only able to do what its members allow and finance it to do. Peacekeeping missions alone have increased exponentially in the last decades and at a time when the United States has become less and less willing to contribute finance or personnel to UN operations. An enhanced role for regional organizations is called for under the umbrella of the UN Security Council. Indeed, by default, this is what has been happening already in the ad hoc responses to crises by so-called 'coalitions of the willing'.

Another possible way forward is for lessons to be learnt from those organizations that have succeeded in bringing governments or national bodies together for small-scale practical tasks addressing particular needs – telecommunications, maritime regulation, banking, etc. Many of these initiatives have grown to take over certain national functions but it has happened gradually, organically and with the full and complete support of the participating parties. Through such initiatives, governments and different sectors of society have come to see that their 'self-interest' can best be served not by a strictly national

approach to problems but only by a concerted international and multilateral approach.

As the UN, EU, NATO, the G8 and, to a lesser extent, the World
Trade Organization struggle to form or reform themselves for effective governance in a global age, there is so much more co-operation
going on across borders – but not in the old-style treaty-based institutionalized ways to which we have become accustomed. Anne-Marie
Slaughter argues that an entire world of inter-governmental (and non-
governmental) networks is flourishing below the radar. As she says
in her book, *A New World Order*, 'networks of government officials
– police investigators, financial regulators, even judges and legislators
– increasingly exchange information and coordinate activity to combat crime and address common problems on a global scale'. We have
seen that to be the case in so many areas of life in the studies earlier in
this book. So one of the major challenges facing our world is how to
allow this bottom-up rather than top-down collaboration to flourish.
How can it flourish in a way that is complementary to and not conflict-
ual with the role of the longer-established bodies?

A brief study of the problem of debt in poorer, developing countries
will show how North and South, governmental and non-governmental
can and do interact in dealing with the challenges of our day. We could
just as easily have used environmental issues and global warming as an
example of the interaction of various players on the international stage,
including the worldwide community of scientists as well as business interests and the investment and insurance industry. In both of these areas
of concern the Christian churches working across national boundaries
and with other faith groups have also played an influential role.

Very little has been said in this book so far specifically about the
debt crisis that has affected large parts of our world for decades and
continues to do so despite huge efforts to deal with it. Over 40 countries are recognized by the International Monetary Fund to be highly
indebted and unable to redress the situation. For most of these countries their debt is unpayable: that is, they struggle to pay even the interest on the debt and do so only by redirecting their scarce financial
resources away from basic services for their own populations.

How did these countries come to be so indebted? That is a long and complicated story but most of these debts were amassed in the 1970s soon after many countries of the South gained their independence. The oil crisis of 1973 pushed the price of oil up very considerably, making many of the oil-rich Arab states very wealthy. Much of this wealth was deposited in western banks which, eager to make it work for them, lent it out on easy terms to governments unused to the workings of the international financial system. The banks themselves paid little attention to whether the countries that borrowed money would be able to repay it. Failure to invest the money productively, worsening rates of exchange for local currencies against the major currencies, cycles of economic boom and bust around the world, together with corruption in some countries meant that many places accumulated a level of debt they could never hope to pay off.

The people who had incurred the debts were not, by and large, the people who suffered the consequences. It was ordinary people who suffered as a result of reduced investment in schools, health services and the creation of employment. Migration from poor southern countries to the north is one consequence of this debt crisis.

It has been the churches in the North that have been the main movers behind trying to cancel this debt burden so as to allow countries to use their own resources for building up their own economies rather than those of the creditor nations in the North. The most prominent campaign was Jubilee 2000. The visionary idea behind this campaign was the brainchild of a retired professor, Martin Dent. He took the biblical idea of Jubilee – a release of people from their debts – which is found in the book of Leviticus and transposed it to the modern day, to the realm of international political debate. His aim for this campaign was that for the Millennium 2000 there should be a cancellation of all the unpayable debt. It was an audaciously ambitious aim to take a biblical principle, which was rarely put into practice in its own time, and translate it into a matter of policy and practice to be taken up by governments and national and international financial institutions.

The campaign took off from its British base to spread to the rest of the developed world and then to the debtor countries themselves.

Links were formed in the United States, which developed its own Jubilee 2000 campaign. Over 60 nations had coalitions of organizations working on the issue. They used all the armoury of modern media to publicize their aims and gain support, including the internet and e-mail. Celebrities were brought on board and taken on tours of Africa to see the impact of debt for themselves. The most impressive show of civil society strength was at the Birmingham G8 meeting in May 1998 when a crowd of 70,000 encircled the city centre.

All this activity for the ending of unpayable debt found a response in people like Gordon Brown and Tony Blair, who carried the message to their peers in the EU and the G8. Breakfast meetings at No. 11 Downing Street between the Chancellor and his officials and the Jubilee 2000 campaigners were frequent occurrences, at which the Chancellor called upon the churches to harness their international networks to bring pressure on EU or G8 countries reluctant to think seriously about the world debt crisis.

Unpayable debt has not all been cancelled but more progress was made than anyone could have imagined. Initiatives still continue within the UN, such as the Millennium Development Goals, which derived their inspiration from this networked campaigning by the churches and civil society both north and south of the equator.

The questions we have raised are urgent and touch our everyday lives. As we have seen, they present us with one challenge after another. While it will be important to find satisfactory solutions to the various problems we've described, just as much attention needs to be given to the processes and methodologies by which we reach them. Our tried and trusted methods seem no longer to work efficiently. They are posited upon assumptions that no longer command confidence. They draw their inspiration from a world order that no longer exists. We have to think 'outside the box'. It's time to identify a new starting place for a radically different kind of discussion.

In a recent book on preaching (*A Reader on Preaching*, edited by David Day, Jeff Astley and Leslie J. Francis) a chapter written by Walter Brueggemann is entitled 'Preaching as Reimagination'.

Brueggemann argues that the world order rooted in the Enlightenment is now virtually at an end. The assumptions behind the view of the world we associate with Descartes, Locke, Hobbes and Rousseau have now shifted. We can no longer think or talk in terms of an 'autonomy of knowledge'. To aim for the possibility of transforming the world we live in, to win the battle for hearts and minds, safe space has to be created where the ambiguities of a world being subjected to radical change can be worked out. It will be space within which we recognize that old assumptions need to be tested for their continuing value while new ones can be discussed and 'owned' by the main actors in our global drama, and all on the basis of trust. Such a process can only be described as 'reimagination'.

Something like this must have happened in the days of the prophet Isaiah. He too had to reimagine the fundamentals of the narrative that had shaped his people. No longer were the assumptions that had thus far undergirded the constant retellings of that story sufficient to meet the realities that faced the prophet in his own day. His efforts are truly breathtaking in his readiness to see the peculiar vocation of his people not in terms of a self-authenticating chosenness, setting them apart from the other nations of the Middle East, so much as a vocation, a divine impulsion, towards establishing a reign of peace for all the nations. And we also saw a similar readiness on the part of those taking the story of Jesus of Nazareth from a Semitic world into a wider Hellenic world to reimagine what had previously been circumscribed within the bounds of Judaism. In that way, its inner power and energy could make inroads into territory previously unthought of.

A similar approach seems to be central to the most recent book published by Bhikhu Parekh, a political philosopher who has written extensively on questions relating to multiculturalism. In a recent article (*Times Higher Education Supplement*, 24 November 2006) he is quoted as saying:

Cultures can become prisons, and for us to be able to experience freedom we need to imagine ourselves outside of our culture, which we cannot do unless we have access to other cultures. It's what I call an interactionist view of multiculturalism, and that interaction creates a space in which we are able to decide what we want to make of ourselves.

It's clear from this just how close the thinking of Parekh and Brueggemann is. Both stress the need for imaginative ways forward and both refer to the need to create new space from which we can view the possibilities facing us at such times as these. They stress the need for individual and collective engagement in intercultural dialogue and somehow to take the discussion of issues identified there beyond the 'deeply engrained defensive barriers between cultures'.

Our efforts in this book have been along similar lines. We've tried to describe a world which, despite everything that subjects the whole planet to forces and factors that affect us all, is suffering an increasing fragmentation. People are trapped in the prisons of cultures and ideologies that cannot of themselves change either the world or the human condition. To address such a situation, we have wanted to draw deeply on the wells of our own Christian faith in order to reimagine the world around us. And it's as Christians that we want to enter the safe space where, with people of other convictions and viewpoints, we'll search for those modalities and methodologies that will become our tools for fashioning a new future. We enter that space with the dignity of our own distinct identity. How we'll come out of it we cannot know. It feels like an adventure. Indeed, it is an adventure. And we invite our readers to join us on it.

Bibliographical Notes

We decided to write this book without footnotes but no reader will remain unaware of the great debt we owe to a number of authors whose thinking has resourced our own. So this note seeks to pay full acknowledgement to those whose writings we have used.

1 The End of an Age

While most of this chapter is a presentation of material culled from the daily press, a reference is made to one or two items that helped to focus our analysis. Rowan Williams' *Writing in the Dust* (London, Hodder and Stoughton, 2002) appeared just before the piece was being written. References to Martin van Creveld's 1986 book *On Future War* and Rupert Smith's more recent *The Utility of Force* came from an article in *The Tablet* of 5 August 2006 called 'War Without End' by Robert Fox. The quotation from Rebecca West's *Black Lamb and Grey Falcon* was drawn from an article in the *Guardian* of 5 August 2006 entitled 'Journeys into History' by Geoff Dyer.

2 Light to Lighten the Nations

The references to Sir Jonathan Sacks' *The Dignity of Difference* (London, Continuum, 2002) are always taken from the important first edition of his book. He was later obliged to rewrite significant portions of both his Preface and his third chapter entitled 'Exorcizing Plato's Ghost'. Our thinking about the Exodus was triggered by an important article by Erich Zenger, 'The God of Exodus in the Message of the Prophets as Seen in Isaiah', which appeared in the international theological journal *Concilium* 189 (1987). Other material was drawn from Martin Noth's' *Exodus* (London, SCM Press Old Testament Library, 1962) as well as *The New Interpreter's Study Bible* (Nashville, Abingdon 2003).

3 Why Do the Nations Rage?

1 Bosnia

The opening illustration is taken from David Toole's remarkable *Waiting for Godot in Sarajevo*, published in London by SCM Press in 2001. Brendan Simm's *Unfinest Hour: Britain and the Destruction of Bosnia* (Harmondsworth, Penguin, 2001) has been an invaluable source for this section, as has *SOS Bosnia* by Adrian Hastings (Leeds, Margaret Fenton Ltd, third edition, 1994).

2 East Timor

The main sources here were Arnold S. Kohen, *From the Place of the Dead: The epic struggles of Bishop Bello of East Timor* (New York, St Martin's Press, 1999) and the relevant chapter of *A Review of Peace Operations: A case for change*, published by The Conflict, Security and Development Group, International Policy Institute, Kings College London in 2003.

3 Eritrea

Michela Wrong's *I Didn't Do It For You: How the world betrayed a small African nation* (London, Harper Perennial, 2005) offers a poignant and passionate analysis of the evolution of events in Eritrea. *Without Troops and Tanks: Humanitarian Intervention in Ethiopia and Eritrea* by Mark Duffield and John Prendergast (Lawrenceville, NJ, Red Sea Press, 1994) illustrates the contribution of Christian Aid and other NGOs to the humanitarian aid supplied to the Eritrean People's Liberation Front during the critical years of its struggle.

4 Haiti

The Aristide Factor by Leslie Griffiths (Oxford, Lion, 1996) provided much of the information here. Robert Fatton's *Haiti's Predatory Republic: The unending transition to democracy* (London, Rienner, 2002) and *Haiti: Human rights investigation November 11–21 2004* by Thomas M. Griffin (Miami, University of Miami School of Law, 2004) have also been most useful.

5 Iraq

Two important books appeared in the immediate aftermath of the 1991 Iraq war. They were contentious in some quarters but undoubtedly gave a graphic picture of life under Saddam Hussein: *Republic of Fear: The inside story of Saddam's Iraq* by Samir al-Khalil (London, Hutchinson Radius, 1990) and *Cruelty and Silence: War, tyranny, uprising, and the Arab world* by Kanan Makiya (London, Jonathan Cape, 1992). Despite the two different names, both books were written by the same person, the first being under a nom de plume. A third book of some consequence was *Saddam Hussein: An American obsession* by Andrew Cockburn and Patrick Cockburn (London, Verso, 2002). We also used an illustration from Ian McEwan's novel *Saturday* (London, Jonathan Cape, 2005).

6 Rwanda

The main inspiration for this section was undoubtedly *We Wish to Inform You That Tomorrow We Will Be Killed with Our Families: Stories from Rwanda* by Philip Gourevitch (New York, Picador, 1998). Gourevitch's book was the basis for the film *Hotel Rwanda* which appeared in 2004.

4 And the Rulers Take Counsel Together

There is a huge range of books on globalization and the following have been particularly helpful in giving the background to this chapter: Manfred B. Steger, *Globalization: A very short introduction* (Oxford, Oxford University Press, 2003); Peter Dicken, *Global Shift: Transforming the World Economy* (London, Paul Chapman, third edition, 1998); David Held, Anthony McGrew, David Goldblatt and Jonathon Perraton, *Global Transformations: Politics, Economics and Culture* (Cambridge, Polity Press, 1999); Saskia Sassen, *Globalization and its Discontents* (New York, The New Press, 1998); David Held and Anthony McGrew, *Governing Globalization: Power, Authority and Global Governance* (Cambridge, Polity Press, 2002).

1 Crime

The following websites were very useful: The Financial Action Tank Force (www.fatf.gafi.org); The United Nations Office on Drugs and Crime (www.unodc.org); The UK Serious Organized Crime Agency (www.soca.gov.uk).

On the trafficking of women and girls, we found Victor Malarek's *The Natasha's: The New Global Sex Trade* (London, Ontario, Viking, 2003) very helpful.

2 Environment

Mark Maslin, *Global Warming: A very short introduction* (Oxford, Oxford University Press, 2004); Mark Lynas, *High Tide: News from a Warming World* (London, Flamingo, 2004); Bjørn Lomborg, *The Skeptical Environmentalist: Measuring the real state of the world* (Cambridge, Cambridge University Press, 2001); Churches Together in Britain and Ireland, *Prosperity with a purpose: Exploring the Ethics of Affluence* (CTBI, 2005).

3 Finance

Ron van Drimmelen, *Faith in a Global Economy: A Primer for Christians* (Geneva, WCC Publications, 1998); Vincent Cable, *Globalization and Global Governance* (London, Royal Institute of International Affairs, 1999); *Understanding Global Issues, Asia's Financial Crisis: Causes, effects and aftershocks* 1998/11 and *Money Across Frontiers: The Explosion of Global Finance* 1999/3 (Cheltenham, Understanding Global Issues).

4 Health

The following websites provided the bulk of the background information for this section: The World Health Organization (www.who.org); Christian Medical Fellowship (www.cmf.org.uk); Médecins sans Frontières (www.msf.org); Drugs for Neglected Diseases (www.dndi.org); Global Alliance for Vaccines and Immunization (www.gavialliance.org).

5 Media

Ian Hargreaves, *Journalism: A very short introduction* (Oxford, Oxford University Press, 2005); Thomas L. McPhail, *Global Communications: Theories, Stakeholders and Trends* (Oxford, Blackwell, second edition, 2006); Chris Arthur, *The Globalization of Communications: Some Religious Implications* (Geneva, WCC Publications, 1998)

Material from the World Summit on the Information Society (www.wsis-cs.org) and from Reporters without borders (www.rsf.org) was equally useful.

6 Migration

Stephen Castles and Mark J Miller, *The Age of Migration: International Population Movements in the Modern World* (Basingstoke, Palgrave Macmillan, third edition, 2003)

Documentation from the Global Commission on International Migration (GCIM) (www.gcim.org) and from the International Organization for Migration (IOM) (www.un.int/iom) was particularly useful.

5 How Long, O Lord, How Long?

Richard Dawkins' book *The God Delusion* was published by Bantam Press in London in 2006. There are many works that treat the nature of Christian fundamentalism. One that we have found particularly useful is Michael Northcott's *An Angel Directs the Storm: Apocalyptic Religion and American Empire*, published in London by I. B. Tauris in 2004 and by SCM Press in 2007. Kenneth Cracknell's book, *In Good and Generous Faith: Christian Responses to Religious Pluralism* was published by Epworth in 2005. Charles Jones' article 'War Within Reason: Not Just War' appeared in the July 2006 number of *Cambridge*.

In addition to the material produced by the United Nations, two books coming from the Princeton University Press have been especially helpful: Anne-Marie Slaughter: *A New World Order* (Princeton, 2004) and Saskia Sassen: *Territory, Authority, Rights: From Medieval to Global Assemblages* (Princeton, 2006).

A Reader on Preaching: Making Connections, edited by David Day, Jeff Astley and Leslie J. Francis, was published in Aldershot by Ashgate in 2005. Professor Biku Parekh's *Reason and Identity* is forthcoming in 2007. He has provided seminal thinking over a number of years in the area of multiculturalism in modern Britain.